CABLE KNITS FROM NORDIC LANDS

BEAUTY AND INGENUITY IN OVER 20 UNIQUE PATTERNS

IVAR ASPLUND

TRAFALGAR SQUARE
North Pomfret, Vermont

First published in the United States of America
in 2019 by
Trafalgar Square Books
North Pomfret, Vermont 05053

Originally published in Swedish as *Sticka Flätor*.

Copyright © 2017 Ivar Asplund and Bonnier Fakta
English translation © 2019 Trafalgar Square Books

The instructions and material lists in this book were carefully reviewed
by the author and editor; however, accuracy cannot be guaranteed. The
Author and publisher cannot be held liable for errors.

ISBN: 978-1-57076-929-0

Library of Congress Control Number: 2019905526

PATTERN INSTRUCTIONS AND TEXT: IVAR ASPLUND
PHOTOGRAPHY: TINA AXELSSON
INTERIOR GRAPHICS: MIKAEL ENGBLOM
EDITOR OF THE SWEDISH EDITION: ANNIKA STRÖM
TRANSLATION INTO ENGLISH: CAROL HUEBSCHER RHOADES

CHARTS CREATED WITH INTERTWINED PATTERN STUDIO

CONTACT, PATTERN QUESTIONS, AND MORE KNITTING:
WWW.ASPLUNDKNITS.BLOGSPOT.SE

Printed in China

10 9 8 7 6 5 4 3 2 1

CONTENTS

PREFACE

PATERNAL GRANDMOTHER
ANNA-STINA

KNITTING has accompanied me almost my whole life. My paternal grandmother, Anna-Stina, showed me the basics when I was five years old, and even though it's difficult to discern which are actual memories and which are moments I've imagined later on, I dare say I was smitten right away. Because we didn't live near each other, we didn't meet very often during the year. So I had to learn mostly on my own, partly by reading handcrafting books and partly by trial-and-error. Grandmother knitted many garments for her children and grandchildren, and she mastered several pattern techniques. I was always examining her projects and asking her to explain how she'd made them. I remember, for example, a white sweater with cables that piqued my curiosity—and, as so often happened, she showed me the techniques weren't as complicated as they seemed.

Cables are rewarding, useful, and fun to knit in so many ways and the basic principles aren't complicated. Simply put, a few stitches change places before they're knitted. The options for variations are endless: the number of stitches involved, the number of rows between cable crossing rows, using just knit stitches or a combination of knit and purl... along with the usual knitting decisions about fiber, color, and needle size. (See more about these decisions on pages 33 and 151).

Grandmother once told me about a time when she'd been upset over a sweater she was working on, when she was young. She wasn't satisfied, ripped it out, and started over. The pattern was complicated and had taken a long time to knit, even when it went well—and it had stopped going well. Her mother told her no one needed to know how long it took to knit; they'd only see how nice the result was. I latched onto that idea. and over time I've realized that it can be interpreted two different ways: yes, it can be worth several hours' extra work to be satisfied ... but it's also possible for a pattern to look more complicated than it is. The beauty and complexity of the result won't necessarily tell you anything about how difficult—or how quick!—the work may have been.

In writing this book, I've had the latter interpretation in the back of my mind; I've done my best to create garments that are easier to knit than you might guess at first glance. The reversible scarf is a good example of a piece that looks complicated—half the fun of knitting it is discovering how simple it really is.

Other garments are, of course, more difficult to knit than that one, but I've tried to make them progress as logically as possible in terms of sequencing and combining the patterns and fitting them neatly into the garments' shaping. It remains to be seen whether what is logical to me is also logical to others!

Personally, I just can't leave things alone when it comes to knitting. I knit often, usually following patterns written by others, but I inevitably change some details along the way (with varying results, I'll admit). In line with my own tendencies, I'm just as happy whether you want to take liberties with these instructions or follow them precisely. The designs reflect my own taste; for example, I've never liked sweaters that draw in at the lower edge, and so there are more straight lower edges and split hems in this book. However, if you prefer ribbed lower edges that fit more closely, feel free to work one that way instead—or adjust anything else that catches your eye.

Finally, I want to share one of my grandmother's sayings with you. She always wanted me to try things for myself; but it made me a little nervous when I was younger, not knowing what might go wrong if I deviated from the instructions. "There is always going to be something a little 'squirrely'," said Grandmother. Obviously I had to see what she meant by that! There have been many small (and large) squirrely challenges over the years, but I'm thankful for them, considering how much I learned from those experiments.

Grandmother died when I was 17 years old, but she continues to be with me in all my projects, because handwork was how we always talked to each other—and she was with me in the making of this book.

IVAR ASPLUND

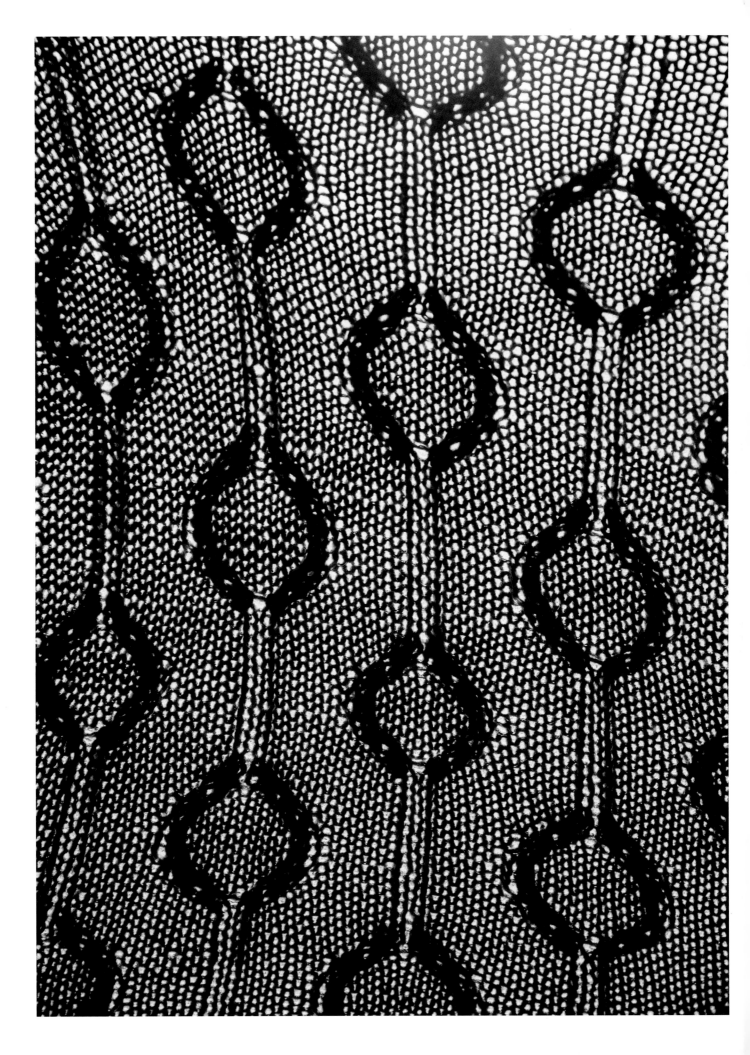

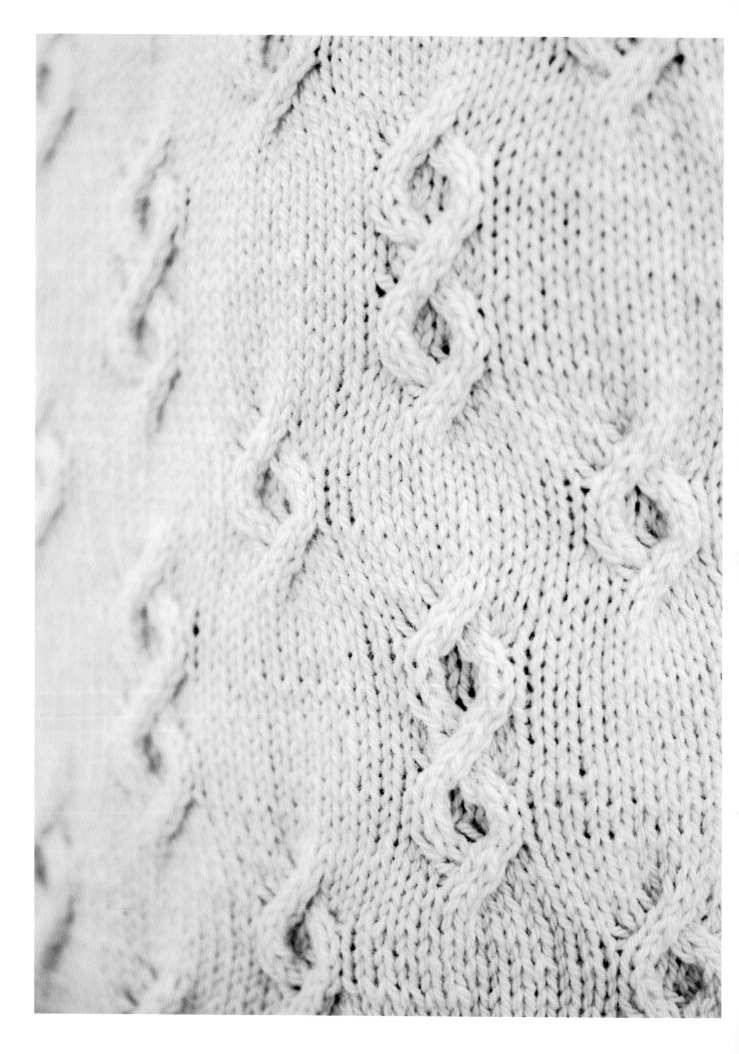

BASIC INFORMATION—
READ BEFORE YOU KNIT!

SIZING

Sizing in these patterns is approximate, so it's a good idea to review all the given measurements in order to choose the right size for you. I think of many of the garments as unisex, such as the Appearances Can Deceive Sweater and the Figure Eights Vest. Often, a "women's medium" can also be considered a "men's small," or vice versa. My best suggestion is to measure a garment that fits you well, and then pick the size from the pattern that comes as close as possible to those measurements.

GAUGE

Gauge (UK tension) plays a role in the garment's overall look and size. Loosely knitted patterns may come out indistinct and shapeless, while tightly knitted pieces might be uncomfortably inflexible. The tension of your knitting is a little like your handwriting—it's much easier to change needle sizes than to try and change your way of doing things.

These days it's easy to find quarter-numbered needles (such as 2.75 and 3.25 mm) in Europe or, in the U.S., half sizes equivalent to 2.5 or 3 mm, which I think makes it easier. Even if a quarter-size or half-size doesn't seem like much, it can make a big difference in a knitted project, not least when it comes to fine needles or many stitches in larger garments such as sweaters and cardigans.

It can be difficult to check your gauge when working cable patterns, because the cables cause the knitted fabric to draw in. For that reason, in this book, I list the gauge as the number of stitches per 4 inches /

10 centimeters in stockinette stitch (stocking stitch). So you need to work your gauge swatch in stockinette to make sure your gauge is correct for the pattern. If you've knitted the swatch too loosely (there are fewer stitches in your measured 4 in / 10 cm than listed for the pattern), then you should try smaller needles. If, on the other hand, you have too many stitches, try larger needles. If you can't match the given gauge exactly, it isn't necessarily a problem—you might want a garment that's a bit larger or a bit smaller than the listed sizes.

Because the gauge is given in stockinette, it should be easier to substitute yarn, as that's how gauge is typically listed on ball bands. I've tried to use common yarn weights, too, which should also make substitutions easier. For example, both Cascade 220 and Renemo (from the Östergötland mill in Sweden) have 218 yd / 200 m in 100 g, so they can be readily substituted for each other. For more information about the yarns used in the designs in this book, see page 156.

YARN AMOUNTS

One of the many wonderful things about cable patterns is the "built-in" ribbing effect (see photo on page 63). You can knit cables instead of ribbing on mitten and sock cuffs. However, for the same reason, it can be risky to substitute cables for stockinette (stocking stitch) in a sweater pattern, because the garment will be too small. The difference will be obvious if you change from cables to stockinette on the same gauge swatch.

THE SAME YARN AND PATTERN WORKED WITH NEEDLES
U.S. 2.5, 3.5, AND 8 / 3, 4, AND 5 MM

CABLES AND STOCKINETTE ON THE SAME GAUGE SWATCH

Because cables draw the fabric in, you'll need more yarn to knit a garment with cables than you would to knit a garment of the same overall size without them. It's hard to say precisely exactly how much more yarn you'll need, but a simple saying holds that "the more cables, the more yarn." More yarn, in turn, means a heavier garment. A cotton sweater, already a heavy fiber, will be even heavier with cables—not just to wear, but to hold while you knit it.

KNITTING IN THE ROUND VS. BACK AND FORTH

Several of the garments are worked back and forth, either completely or partially. Knitting in the round is practical, but it's often easier to work cables back and forth. Knitting back and forth, it's possible for the cable crossings to fall only on right-side facing rows, which makes it easy to keep track of them; with circular knitting, you'd have to pay constant attention to whether you're on a "return" round or not.

It's also difficult to count rows in cable knitting. When the patterns are worked in the round, I've tried to add an element to make it easier—for example, seed stitch/UK moss stitch, or another pattern with easy-to-count rounds.

As far as needles are concerned, I find it the most practical to work with circular needles, because they can be used to knit both back and forth and in the round. If you prefer straight needles, you can use them for the garments or the parts of a garment not worked in the round, even if it doesn't state that in the instructions. I do recommend circular needles for garments with a high stitch count, such as for the Free and Easy Top, the Triple Triangles Shawl, the Wrought Iron Cardigan, and the button bands on the X & O Cardigan. Likewise, you can substitute a long magic-loop circular for a set of double-pointed needles, even if the instructions don't say so.

CASTING ON AND EDGE STITCHES

When casting on for these garments, I generally use the long-tail cast-on (with one strand around the thumb and another around the index finger), but you can use other methods if you prefer. If you want to try a different cast-on, read the garment instructions first to find out whether the first row is worked from the right or wrong side, so you can decide which side of your cast-on should be visible.

When working garment pieces back and forth, it's a good idea to add edge stitches for seaming. There are several options for edge stitches and each knitter has her favorite method. Personally, I like to have two edge stitches on each side, which I make as follows: At the beginning of every row, I slip the first stitch purlwise with the yarn in front and then knit the second stitch. I knit the last two stitches at the end of each row.

But, of course, you should feel free to use a different method! The edges will lie on the inside of the finished garment and won't be visible, so pick any technique that works for you. If an edge will be visible, as for the edges of a placket or split hem, I use a different technique for edge stitches. Those exceptions will be explained in the individual pattern instructions.

AN ALMOST COMPLETED SLEEVE SEAM TO END AT THE UNDERARM SHAPING

GAUGE SWATCH WITH CABLE TURNS AND EDGE STITCHES

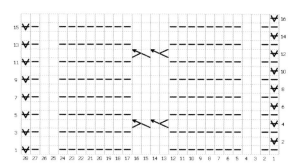

STITCHES ARE NUMBERED FROM RIGHT TO LEFT (= THE DIRECTION OF KNITTING)

READING CHARTS

At first glance, a chart can look downright confusing, with so many different symbols and numbers (see the Symbol explanations on page 157), but charts can actually make knitting easier. Charts are drawn to resemble the knitted fabric to as great a degree as possible. For example, an empty square symbolizes a knit stitch on the right side (RS). If you're working in the round, all the empty squares represent knit stitches on the RS because you always have the right side facing. If you are working back and forth, the empty squares are purled on alternate rows (which is to say on the wrong side, or WS) so they will be visible as knit stitches on the RS of the piece.

The placement of the row numbers will indicate whether you should work back and forth or in the round. If all the numbers are on the right side of the chart, you should work in the round and read the chart from right to left throughout. If the numbers alternate between the right and left sides of the chart, you will work back and forth beginning on the side indicated by the row number. Red lines on a chart surround a repeat; the stitches and rows that are repeated will be enclosed.

> **KNITTING TIP:** Lay a ruler or use a row marker on the chart to make it easy to follow the rows. If you place the ruler directly above the row to be worked, it'll be easier to compare the chart with your knitting. If you lay the ruler below the row to be worked, it will hide the rows you've completed.

SWATCH THE PATTERN

If cable knitting is a new technique for you, test it out with the swatch and chart above. Begin by casting on 28 stitches.

The row numbers alternate between the right and left sides of the chart.

Row 1: Begin on the WS, reading the chart from left to right (the symbols are mirror-image). Sl 1 purlwise, k1, p2, k8, p4, k8, p2, k2.

Row 2: Work on the RS, reading the chart from right to left: Sl 1 purlwise, knit to end of row.

Row 3 and all odd-numbered rows: Work as for Row 1.
Row 4: Work as for Row 2, but cross the cable at the center: Sl 1 purlwise, k11, cable 4 sts = place 2 sts on a cable needle and hold in front of work, k2, k2 from cable needle; k12.
Row 12: Work as for Row 4; work remaining even-numbered rows as for Row 2.

WASHING AND BLOCKING GARMENTS

I actually think one of the high points of knitting a garment is washing and blocking it. You might be so pleased with the garment that you want to wear it right away, but it's still a good idea to wash it first. No matter how careful you are while knitting, it's inevitable that the piece will get a little dirty as you work. Blocking will also help even out the garment by allowing the fibers to align better. An even, smooth surface makes a garment doubly pretty.

Different yarns need different care, so be sure to follow the washing instructions recommended for that yarn. Last but not least: Only let someone you really trust wash your handknit garments (perhaps the ultimate test of confidence?).

A knitted garment that's wet or damp can be shaped in certain ways, especially if it's knitted with wool yarn. I usually try on the garment before washing it to see if it sits well or needs adjustment. If the sleeves are a bit too short and wide, I know that I can pull them enough to lengthen them. Usually I have another sweater that fits well to use as a template for the newly knitted piece.

Some knitters wash and block the garment pieces first and save the assembly for last. I normally do the opposite, mostly just to have the finishing over and done with. I also find it easier to block a complete sweater or cardigan, especially because I can turn it inside out. That way, the seams and picked-up joins are visible and I can align and adjust them as the garment dries.

A BASIC TECHNIQUE FOR JOINING TWO PIECES

FINISHING

Something I share with many other knitters is a resistance
to sewing the pieces together. For that reason, I usually
join pieces by knitting them together with three-needle
bind-off. Instead of binding off the shoulders and then
sewing the front and back pieces together, I leave the
live stitches on an extra needle or scrap yarn (use smooth
cotton yarn rather than wool, because wool can felt; the
cotton yarn will easily slide out of the live stitches).

To join the pieces, I place them together (usually with
RS facing RS), holding the needles parallel as shown
above: Knit 2 together (one stitch from each needle).
Knit the next two stitches together and pass the first st
on right needle over the last knitted. For step-by-step
instructions, see page 134. This method is called "three-
needle bind-off" because you need three needles: one
for each piece and one for knitting. If you work this bind-
off with the wrong sides facing out, it joins the patterns
smoothly; with the right side out, a decorative edge is
formed. In this book, I've used both options—the former
appears on the Wrought Iron Cardigan (see page 112)

and the latter on the Appearances Can Deceive Sweater
(see page 80), just to take two examples.

PICKING UP STITCHES FOR THE SLEEVES

My favorite way to knit sleeves is to pick up and knit
stitches along the edge and work each sleeve directly
onto the garment. Of course, that way can be a little
heavy and unwieldy to work with. However, after you've
worked enough of the sleeve to give yourself some slack,
you don't need to turn the entire piece around but can
let it lie like a cat on your knee, and only turn the sleeve
(if you're knitting back and forth). It's also easy to try on
the garment this way, sleeves included; you can check
the width and length of the sleeve, and decide whether
you'll need to adjust the number of decreases or make
the sleeve longer or shorter than it is in the instructions.

It's important to remember that stitches are
rectangular and not square. For that reason, I don't pick
up a stitch every row, but rather three stitches every four
rows. Alternatively, you could pick up a stitch every row
and then decrease the stitch count on the first row.

Don't forget the edge stitches! I like to have edge stitches for seaming, but this means I have to separate them from the stitches that are picked up in order to be able to fold them out of the way completely when I sew the seams.

For that reason, I begin by casting on for the edge stitches before I pick up and knit stitches along the armhole (see photo below). I then finish by casting on the edge stiches on the other side.

The sleeves can also be knitted separately and then attached. In that case, add a couple of extra rows for seaming.

SIDE SEAMS AND MATTRESS STITCH

A simple way to join the side and sleeve seams is to use mattress stitch (see page 135). Hold the right sides facing and zigzag upwards. With two edge stitches at each side, I sew into the third stitch column, which is inside the edge stitches. This makes a relatively wide seamline, but the edges are folded to the wrong side and won't be particularly lumpy. I usually sew into each stitch at the beginning and end of the seam, and then between two at a time the rest of the way, because it makes the seaming faster and I don't see a big difference in the results, at least when the garment is worked in one color. Try it out—it's easy to pull the yarn out if you aren't happy with the results. This method is easiest with a bent-tip tapestry needle.

WHY CABLES?

Why does anyone choose to knit cables? If you want your knitting to look like woven fabric as much as possible, then cables are absolutely the wrong technique. However, if you want a warm, elastic, eye-catching knitted garment, cables are a fantastic option. Many cable patterns are constructed with stockinette columns against a purl background, so there's a ribbing effect. Crossing the cables draws in the fabric even more—an elegant way to combine form and function.

You can knit cables as a purely decorative element, particularly if you agree with me that they're a lot of fun to knit. I'm not just thinking about the structural effect when I place a cable pattern over, for example, the back of a sweater or cardigan. In the pattern samples on page 139 and following, you'll find suggestions for several pattern shapes to use in your own creations. For almost inexhaustible resources, I warmly recommend that you immerse yourself in the rich and ingeniously patterned sweaters from Guernsey and the Aran Islands.

TOOLS

On the next two pages, you'll see pictures of several useful tools. These days, there are quite a few equipment options to buy, but I like to use what I already have. You don't need to buy all sorts of markers; you can use regular safety pins instead. A broken circular, a short double-pointed needle, or a straight tapestry needle can all substitute for a cable needle in a pinch.
I also think a bent-tip tapestry needle is a good investment because it makes finishing easy. When blocking pieces, I use T-pins—they're easier to grip than regular straight pins.

If you have made a shawl, blocking wires can be practical to use (not shown).

PICK UP AND KNIT STITCHES BY BRINGING THE YARN THROUGH THE PIECE

SIDE SEAM: SEW ALL THE WAY OR LEAVE A SPLIT OPENING

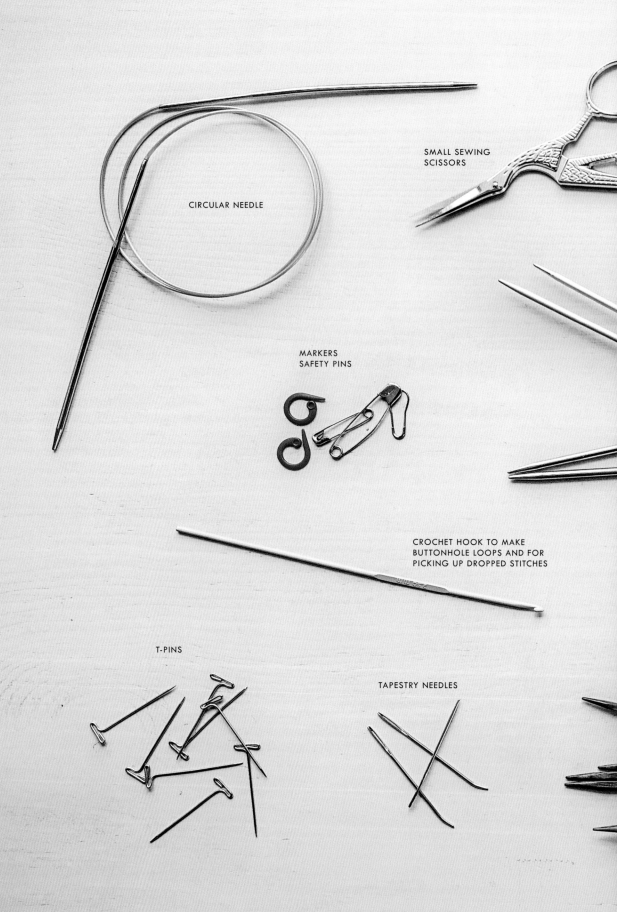

CIRCULAR NEEDLE

SMALL SEWING
SCISSORS

MARKERS
SAFETY PINS

CROCHET HOOK TO MAKE
BUTTONHOLE LOOPS AND FOR
PICKING UP DROPPED STITCHES

T-PINS

TAPESTRY NEEDLES

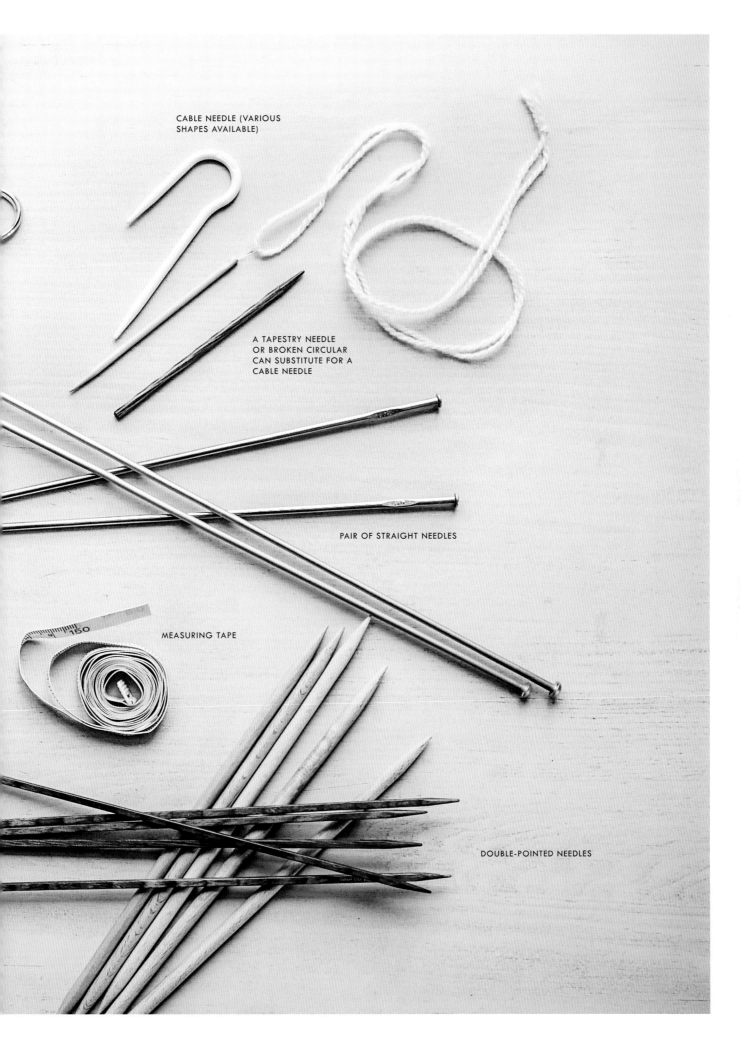

CABLE NEEDLE (VARIOUS SHAPES AVAILABLE)

A TAPESTRY NEEDLE OR BROKEN CIRCULAR CAN SUBSTITUTE FOR A CABLE NEEDLE

PAIR OF STRAIGHT NEEDLES

MEASURING TAPE

DOUBLE-POINTED NEEDLES

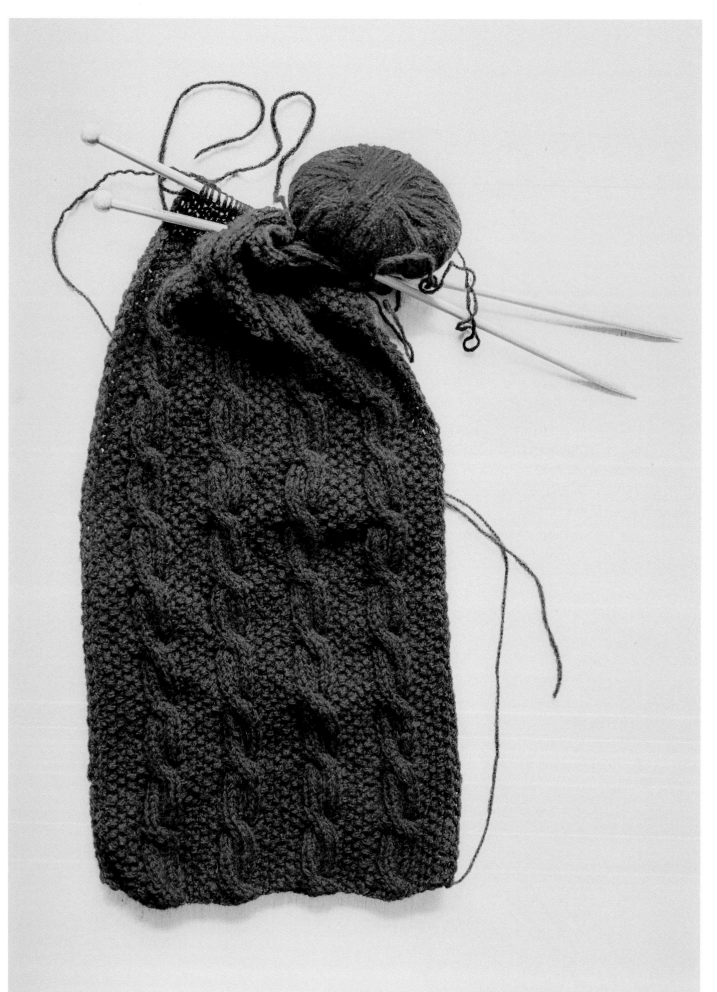

PATTERN INSTRUCTIONS

Delight in variety! Among the patterns, you'll find several types of garments, with a variety of patterns and construction methods. They are arranged, more or less, in order from easiest to most challenging. Those I think are easy might still be a challenge for someone else, of course. If there's anything special about a pattern, I discuss that in the introductory text—it might be a step that needs extra concentration or a solution for making the knitting easier.

At the beginning of every pattern, you'll find an actual size yarn sample and, on page 156, information about all the different yarns used in the book.

A Symbols Key for all the charts is located on page 157.

APÉRITIF WRIST WARMERS

SKILL LEVEL INTERMEDIATE
SIZE ONE SIZE (LENGTH AS DESIRED)

MATERIALS
YARN:
CYCA #3 (SPORT) ÖSTERGÖTLANDS
ULLSPINNERI VISJÖ (100% WOOL, 328
YD/300 M / 100 G)
YARN AMOUNT AND COLOR:
1 SKEIN IN YOUR CHOICE OF COLOR

NEEDLES U.S. SIZE 4 / 3.5 MM: PAIR OF
STRAIGHT NEEDLES; CABLE NEEDLE
GAUGE
22 STS IN ST ST = 4 IN / 10 CM.
ADJUST NEEDLE SIZE TO OBTAIN
CORRECT GAUGE IF NECESSARY.

EVEN SMALL GARMENTS can make a big difference when it comes to keeping warm. Decorated with cables, these wrist warmers are a quick and straightforward project if you want to try cable knitting for the first time (and you might develop a taste for it). These cuffs are worked back and forth with cable crossings on every other row and only one pattern to keep track of.

I added edge stitches and finished with mattress stitch because both of these techniques are used in several other patterns—it's a good idea to try them out on a small project first.

There are two edge stitches at each side, worked the same way on every row: slip the first stitch as if to purl with the yarn held in front. Knit the second stitch and knit the last two stitches of the row.

APÉRITIF WRIST WARMERS

CO 50 sts. If you leave a long tail, you can use it for seaming later. Work back and forth following the chart. (For extra clarity, the first two rows of the chart have been written out below.) See page 157 for the Symbols Key.

Row 1 (WS): Sl 1 purlwise, k1, p2, *k3, p6, k3, p3*; work from * to * a total of 2 times. K3, p6, k3, p2, k2.
Row 2 (RS): Sl 1 purlwise, k3, *p3, k6, p3, k3*; work from * to * a total of 2 times and end p3, k6, p3, k4.
Row 3 and all odd-numbered rows: Work as for Row 1.

Work the 27 charted rows or to desired length. With RS facing, BO, working knit over knit and purl over purl to maintain the elasticity. Knit the last 2 sts together through back loops so the corner won't be too loose. Seaming will be easier if you wash and block the wrist warmers before you seam them. Make sure there's enough yarn from either the cast-on or bind-off to sew the seams—that leaves fewer ends to weave in. You'll need a length of yarn about 1½ times the length at the sides.

Join the sides with mattress stitch (see page 135). With RS facing, sew zigzag fashion in the center of the outermost St st columns (= the third stitch as counted from the beginning or end of the chart). That way, you'll form a three-stitch-wide St st column to match those between the cables.

1 STS + 1½ STS = 3 STITCHES IN WIDTH

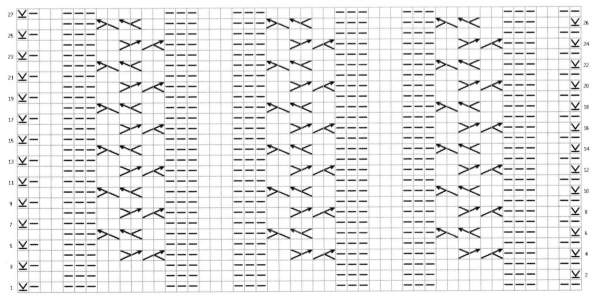

THE CHART SHOWS ALL THE STITCHES AND ROWS FOR THE WRIST WARMER. THE REPEAT IN LENGTH IS ONLY 4 ROWS (ROWS 4-7).

TWIST AND TURN SCARF

SKILL LEVEL INTERMEDIATE
SIZE SMALL (LARGE)
FINISHED MEASUREMENTS
WIDTH: 6¼ (9½) IN / 16 (24) CM
LENGTH: 47¼ (75) IN / 120 (190) CM

MATERIALS
YARN:
CYCA #3 (SPORT) LANG NOVA (48%
MERINO WOOL, 32% CAMEL, 20% NY-
LON, 197 YD/180 M / 25 G)
YARN AMOUNT AND COLOR:
2 (5) BALLS COLOR 39 (22)

NEEDLES U.S. SIZE 10 / 6 MM: PAIR OF
STRAIGHT NEEDLES; CABLE NEEDLE
NOTIONS ROW COUNTER AND/OR
STITCH MARKERS (OPTIONAL)
GAUGE
16 STS IN ST ST = 4 IN / 10 CM.
ADJUST NEEDLE SIZE TO OBTAIN
CORRECT GAUGE IF NECESSARY.

IT'S ADVANTAGEOUS for scarves to have matching patterns on each side—
for example, seed stitch/UK moss stitch. Or, in this case, reversible cables. It's
surprisingly easy to knit them! Think about ribbing; say, two knit and two purl
stitches, repeated. It looks the same on both sides when the piece is turned.
If you cross cables in that kind of ribbing, the cables will also be the same on
both sides. No right or wrong sides!

   The only tricky aspect of this project is keeping track of the number of rows
between cable crosses. Use a method or tool that works for you—for example,
markers or a row counter.

   For neat, flexible edges, I chose to work as follows with the two outermost
stitches at each side: At the beginning of the row, slip them purlwise with yarn
held in front, and, at the end of the row, knit the last two stitches.

TWIST AND TURN SCARF

CO 48 (74) sts. No chart is needed for this pattern as all the rows (except for the cable crossings beginning on Row 3) are worked the same way:

Non-Cable Crossing Rows: Sl 2 sts purlwise wyf, *k1, p1, k1, p1, k3, p2, k2, p2*; rep * to * until 7 sts rem. End with k1, p1, k1, p1, k3.

Rows 3, 13, 23, etc (= every 10th row) cross cables: Sl 2 purlwise as before, *k1, p1 k1, p1, k1; place 4 sts on cable needle and hold in front of work, k2, p2; k2, p2 from cable needle*; rep until 7 sts rem. End with k1, p1, k1, p1, k3.

After the final cable row, work 1 row as for non-cable crossing rows.

Binding off: Sl 2 as est, k1, and pass the 2 slipped sts over. Continue, binding off in pattern (knit over knit and purl over purl on the cables, and in seed st over seed st/ UK moss stitch) until 2 sts rem on left needle; k2tog tbl to keep the corner from being too loose. Cut yarn and fasten off. Wash scarf carefully and block.

CHANGING THE SIZE

The size of this scarf is easy to adjust. To change the length, simply work more or fewer rows. To adjust the width, work more or fewer repeats—the pattern given here has 3 (5) repeats of 13 sts each.

You can also change the number of stitches in the seed stitch/UK moss stitch columns. You'll need an odd number (5 in the scarves shown here) in each column to ensure both sides will match.

WITH SO MANY STITCHES IN THE CABLE CROSSINGS, THE CABLES WILL BE ESPECIALLY PLUMP

TEST TUBE COWL

SKILL LEVEL INTERMEDIATE
SIZE SMALL (LARGE)
FINISHED MEASUREMENTS
CIRCUMFERENCE: 15¾ (20½) IN /
40 (52) CM, UNSTRETCHED
LENGTH: 6 (6¾) IN / 15 (17) CM,
UNSTRETCHED

MATERIALS
YARN:
SMALL: CYCA #4 (WORSTED, AFGHAN,
ARAN) DE RERUM NATURA GILLIATT
(100% MERINO WOOL, 273 YD/250 M
/ 100 G), 1 BALL CIEL
LARGE: CYCA #4 WORSTED, AFGHAN,
ARAN) DE RERUM NATURA CYRANO

(100% MERINO WOOL, 164 YD/150 M
/ 100 G), 1 BALL LAGOON
NEEDLES U.S. SIZE 8 (10) / 5 (6) MM:
16 IN (40) CM CIRCULAR; CABLE NEEDLE
GAUGE
17 (14) STS IN ST ST = 4 IN / 10 CM.
ADJUST NEEDLE SIZE TO OBTAIN COR-
RECT GAUGE IF NECESSARY.

GILLIATT   CYRANO

I LIKE TO TRY OUT different pattern variations in a single swatch. Partly because that makes it easy to compare the variations, having them right next to each other, and partly because it always gives me new ideas about how to combine patterns with each other and bring out various effects with only small changes.

You can try out several different cable patterns on this cowl, with minimal variation. At the most basic level, it's just two (mirror-image) cable crossings, but they combine in various ways to produce dramatic results. To make things even easier, the cables alternate to the right and left when you knit Row 4 of the chart. Hopefully you'll want to play more with your own variations!

TEST TUBE COWL

BOTH SIZES

With circular for your chosen size, CO 100 sts. Join, being careful not to twist cast-on row—it's so frustrating when you suddenly discover you're working a figure-eight instead of a tube. Pm for beginning of rnd.

Work the 50 sts of the chart twice around. See the Symbols Key on page 157.

Repeat the 8 chart rows 5 (4) times or to desired length. End with Rows 1-3.

BO with knit over knit and purl over purl to maintain the elasticity. Cut yarn; fasten off ends. Gently wash and block.

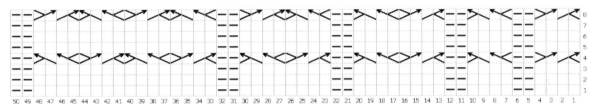

REPEAT ROWS 1—8

THE LENGTH CAN BE EASILY ADJUSTED BY CHANGING THE NUMBER OF REPEATS. THE LARGER SIZE (KNITTED WITH A HEAVIER YARN) HAS 4 REPEATS.

SQUIGGLES HAT

SKILL LEVEL INTERMEDIATE
SIZE CHILD (ADULT)
FINISHED MEASUREMENTS
HEAD CIRCUMFERENCE: 17¼-20½
(20½-23¾) IN / 44-52 (52-60) CM
LENGTH: 8 (9½) IN / 20 (24) CM

MATERIALS
YARN:
CYCA #4 (WORSTED, AFGHAN, ARAN)
CASCADE YARNS CASCADE 220 (100%
PERUVIAN HIGHLAND WOOL, 220
YD/201 M / 100 G)
YARN AMOUNT AND COLOR:
100 G COLOR HEATHERS 9488 (9451)

NEEDLES U.S. SIZE 4 (6) / 3½ (4) MM:
SMALL CIRCULAR AND SET OF 5 DPN;
CABLE NEEDLE
NOTIONS 5 STITCH MARKERS
GAUGE
22 (20) STS IN ST ST ON U.S. 4 (6) /
3½ (4) MM NEEDLES = 4 IN / 10 CM.
ADJUST NEEDLE SIZE TO OBTAIN COR-
RECT GAUGE IF NECESSARY.

THE IDEA FOR THIS PATTERN popped up as I was pondering various ways
to make it easier to knit cable patterns in the round. One solution is making
cables cross on every round. Moving the cables so they only make one
sideways step at a time means that the knitting doesn't draw in too much,
especially when you do this only five times around. And I love a cable pattern
that's a little on the bias!

For this hat, you can follow the same set of instructions, no matter the size
because sizing is determined by the needle size.

SQUIGGLES HAT

Because this hat consists of five repeats, it's easy to divide the stitches onto five double-pointed needles and knit with a sixth. If you use a circular instead, I recommend that you block off each repeat with stitch markers. In either case, divide the stitches as soon as you finish the ribbing. When shaping the crown, change to double-pointed needles when the stitches no longer fit around a circular.

CO 120 sts with gauge-size needles for chosen size. Join, being careful not to twist cast-on row; pm for beginning of rnd. Work around following the chart (see page 157 for Symbols Key).

After completing charted rows, cut yarn and draw end through rem 5 sts. Tighten yarn.

Finishing: Weave in all ends neatly on WS. Hand wash gently in lukewarm water and wool-safe soap.

PIE SLICE SHAPING NEAR THE TOP

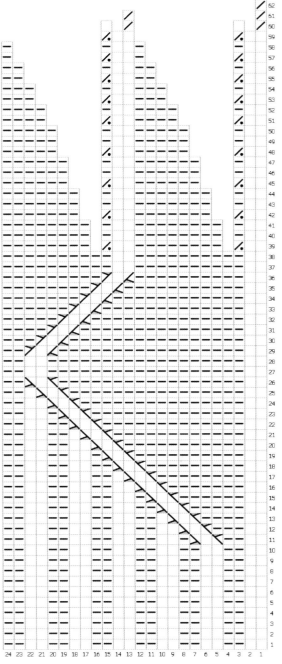

DECREASES LEAVE EMPTY SPACES ON THE CHART

SUPER WRIST WARMERS

SKILL LEVEL INTERMEDIATE
SIZE ONE SIZE (LENGTH AS DESIRED)
MATERIALS
YARN:
CYCA #1 (FINGERING) CAMAROSE

YAKU (100% MERINO WOOL, 219
YD/200 M / 50 G)
YARN AMOUNT AND COLOR:
50 G COLOR 1011 ASH GRAY
NEEDLES U.S. SIZE 1.5 / 2.5 MM: SET

OF 5 DPN; CABLE NEEDLE
GAUGE
28 STS IN ST ST = 4 IN / 10 CM.
ADJUST NEEDLE SIZE TO OBTAIN COR-
RECT GAUGE IF NECESSARY.

THE SPIRAL EFFECT was designed as a decorative way to make the knitting easier. On alternating rounds, you work knit over knit and purl over purl and, on the remaining rounds, cross the cables on every third column.

Because the crossings follow each other, I call these wrist warmers *Super*. (The original Swedish name for this pattern was *Kanon*—"canon"—which in this case has nothing to do with weapons. In Swedish, this means something especially good, and in this case, something good both to knit and to wear.) The same pattern, with its lovely ribbed effect, would be equally effective as cuffs for mittens or socks.

The elasticity of the patterning also means that these wrist warmers will fit a variety of wrist sizes. The photo on the facing page to the right clearly shows how the design looks when stretched around the wrist.

SUPER WRIST WARMERS

With dpn, CO 72 sts. Divide sts onto 4 dpn with 18 sts per needle. Join, being careful not to twist cast-on row; pm for beginning of rnd.

Work the first two rounds following Chart A (see Symbols Key on page 157) and then repeat Rows 3-8 of chart seven times or to desired length. BO in pattern; cut yarn.

Work the second cuff mirror-image following Chart B—or make it exactly as for the first cuff, if you prefer.

Finishing: Weave in all ends neatly on WS. Hand wash gently in lukewarm water and wool-safe soap.

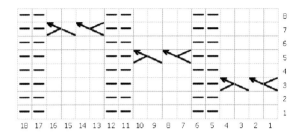

CHART A: LEFT CUFF

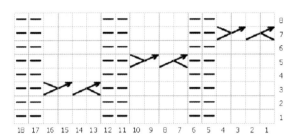

CHART B: RIGHT CUFF

IF YOU TURN THE CUFFS INSIDE OUT, YOU CAN SEE THE RIBBING CLEARLY

CHAIN AND HORSESHOE HAT

SKILL LEVEL INTERMEDIATE
SIZE ADULT SHORT (ADULT LONG)
FINISHED MEASUREMENTS
HEAD CIRCUMFERENCE: 20½-23¾ IN / 52-60 CM
LENGTH: 7½ (9½) IN / 19 (24) CM
MATERIALS
YARN:
CYCA #4 (WORSTED, AFGHAN, ARAN)

CASCADE YARNS CASCADE 220 (100% PERUVIAN HIGHLAND WOOL, 220 YD/201 M / 100 G)
YARN AMOUNT AND COLOR:
100 G COLOR 8401 (9465)
NEEDLES U.S. SIZES 4 AND 6 / 3½ AND 4 MM: 16 IN / 40 CM CIRCULAR OR SET OF 5 DPN (SMALLER SIZE OPTIONAL FOR RIBBING—SEE NOTE AT TOP OF

PAGE 67); CABLE NEEDLE
NOTIONS 6 STITCH MARKERS
GAUGE
20 STS ON LARGER NEEDLES IN ST ST = 4 IN / 10 CM.
ADJUST NEEDLE SIZE TO OBTAIN CORRECT GAUGE IF NECESSARY.

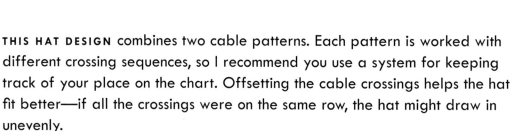

THIS HAT DESIGN combines two cable patterns. Each pattern is worked with different crossing sequences, so I recommend you use a system for keeping track of your place on the chart. Offsetting the cable crossings helps the hat fit better—if all the crossings were on the same row, the hat might draw in unevenly.

As with the Squiggles Hat on page 56, the cable lines run directly from the ribbing for the alternating chain and horseshoe patterns. I'm especially fond of this type of detail.

CHAIN AND HORSESHOE HAT

I actually worked these hats with the same needle size throughout. However, if you want a firmer lower edge, use the smaller set of needles for the ribbing. The chart shows the long version. For the short hat (light gray), work only 6 rounds of ribbing and omit Rows 46-53 of chart.

With your choice of needles for the ribbing, CO 120 sts. Join, being careful not to twist cast-on row; pm for beginning of rnd.

Rep the 20 sts across chart 6 times around (see Symbols Key on page 157).

After completing Row 70 (top of chart), cut yarn and draw end through rem sts and tighten.

Finishing: Weave in all ends neatly on WS. Hand wash gently in lukewarm water and wool-safe soap.

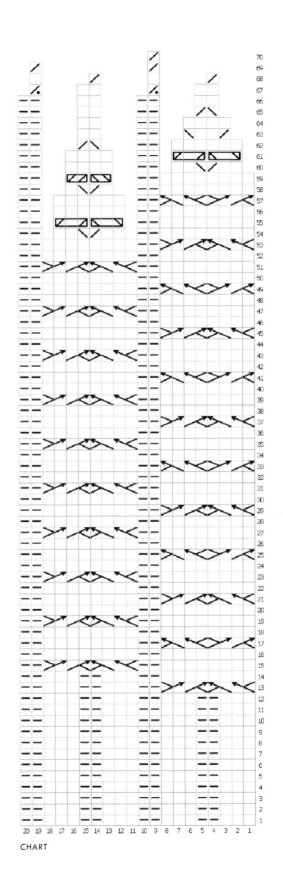

CHART

BY ADDING MORE ROUNDS, YOU CAN MAKE THE HAT POINTIER BECAUSE IT WON'T BE STRETCHED OUT AROUND YOUR HEAD ALL THE WAY UP.

REVERSIBLE FAUX TURTLE

SKILL LEVEL INTERMEDIATE
SIZE ONE SIZE (ADULT)
FINISHED MEASUREMENTS
LENGTH: 13¾ IN / 35 CM
MATERIALS
YARN:
CYCA #4 (WORSTED, AFGHAN, ARAN)
NORDISK ANGORA KARELEN (50%

WOOL, 50% ANGORA RABBIT, 273
YD/250 M / 100 G)
YARN AMOUNT AND COLOR:
100 G WHITE
NEEDLES U.S. SIZE 4 / 3.5 MM: 16 AND
24 IN / 40 AND 60 CM CIRCULARS;
CABLE NEEDLE

NOTIONS ROW COUNTER AND/OR
MARKERS
GAUGE
20 STS IN ST ST = 4 IN / 10 CM.
ADJUST NEEDLE SIZE TO OBTAIN COR-
RECT GAUGE IF NECESSARY.

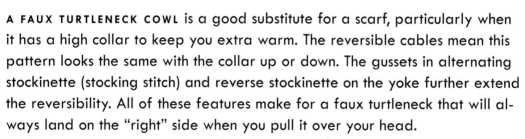

A FAUX TURTLENECK COWL is a good substitute for a scarf, particularly when it has a high collar to keep you extra warm. The reversible cables mean this pattern looks the same with the collar up or down. The gussets in alternating stockinette (stocking stitch) and reverse stockinette on the yoke further extend the reversibility. All of these features make for a faux turtleneck that will always land on the "right" side when you pull it over your head.

This extended cowl is worked from the top down—first as a straight tube, and then with increases for the yoke. This makes it easy to lengthen the yoke if, for example, you want to knit a poncho instead. After a few increase rounds, the stitches won't fit on the short circular, so you can then change to the longer needle.

REVERSIBLE FAUX TURTLE

With short circular, CO 120 sts. Join, being careful not to twist cast-on row; pm for beginning of rnd.

Rnds 1-9: (K2, p2) around.
Rnd 10: *Place 4 sts on cable needle and hold in front of work, k2, p2; k2, p2 from cable needle; k2, p2*; rep * to * 9 more times.
Rep Rnds 1-10 until you've worked a total of 59 rnds.
Rnd 60 (6th cable crossing row): Begin increases (see chart below for placement of increases). Work increases as yarnover (yo) between cables 20 times around. Also, see Symbols Key on page 157.

*Place 4 sts on cable needle and hold in front of work, k2, p2; k2, p2 from cable needle; k1, yo, k1, p1, yo, p1 *; rep * to * 9 more times.

On the following rnd, work yarnover through back loop to avoid an ugly hole. Work yarnovers as k1 tbl between knit sts and p1 tbl between purl sts.

Continue in pattern as est, increasing on every 5th rnd (every other time will be on a cable crossing rnd) through Rnd 90, and then make the 8th increase on Rnd 100 = 280 sts.

Finish with 5 rnds k2, p2 ribbing. The stitch count allows both the gussets and cables to transition as smoothly as possible into the ribbing.

If you want to lengthen the piece with more increases, I recommend that you increase, for example, 4 or 8 more times (to a multiple of 4) if you want to achieve the same smooth transition from pattern to ribbing.

BO in ribbing (knit over knit, purl over purl) to maintain the elasticity.

Finishing: Weave in all ends neatly on WS. Hand wash gently in lukewarm water and wool-safe soap. Block by patting piece out to finished measurements.

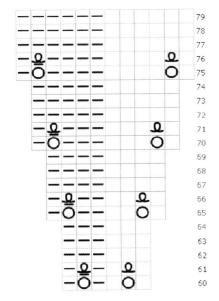

GUIDE FOR INCREASES

TRIPLE TRIANGLES SHAWL

SKILL LEVEL INTERMEDIATE
SIZE ADAPTABLE
**FINISHED MEASUREMENTS BEFORE
BLOCKING**
WIDTH: 25½ (30¾) IN / 65 (78) CM
LENGTH: 13 (15) IN / 33 (38) CM

MATERIALS
YARN:
CYCA #4 (WORSTED, AFGHAN, ARAN)
NORDISK ANGORA KARELEN (50%
WOOL, 50% ANGORA RABBIT, 273
YD/250 M / 100 G)
YARN AMOUNT AND COLOR:
100 G MEDIUM GRAY

NOTIONS BLOCKING WIRES
NEEDLES U.S. SIZE 8 / 5 MM: 32 IN /
80 CM CIRCULAR; CABLE NEEDLE
GAUGE
16 STS IN ST ST = 4 IN / 10 CM
BEFORE BLOCKING.
ADJUST NEEDLE SIZE TO OBTAIN
CORRECT GAUGE IF NECESSARY.

I REALLY LIKE KNITTING SHAWLS and this silhouette is one of my favorites. It's worked outward from the back neck and consists of three triangles, which allows it to sit well over the shoulders and not slide off. It also won't catch in a waistband or belt when put on, because it's horizontal across the back.

To keep it simple, this shawl has just a couple of easy cables, emphasized with yarnover increases on each side to form a decorative lace pattern. Between the cables, alternating sections of garter and moss stitch/UK double moss stitch complete the overall pattern. I've chosen a bind-off method that combines well with the lace. It's not a difficult bind-off, but be prepared to take a little time and make sure you have plenty of yarn—about the same amount as for six rows of knitting.

TRIPLE TRIANGLES SHAWL

Because the shawl is worked from the neck down, it's easy to adjust the size to your liking, or to suit the amount of yarn you've got to work with. With few stitches at the beginning, the first rows are fast to knit, so you can get a running start on the project.

Feel free to choose your yarn quality and needle size when it comes to this design. If you want to knit with finer or thicker yarn, or with other needle sizes, all you have to do is swatch and adjust to match the gauge; that way you can be sure the shawl won't be too narrow under your arms.

CO 21 sts and purl 1 row (set-up) = WS. The next 6 rows are shown on Chart A but you can also check the text version for extra security. See the Symbols Key on page 157.

Row 1: K5, yo, *k1, yo, k4, yo*; rep * to * once more and end k1, yo k5.

Row 2: P5, *k3, p4*; rep * to * once more, end k3, p5.

Row 3: K5, yo, *k3, yo, k4, yo*; rep * to * once more, end k3, yo, k5.

Row 4: P5, *k5, p4*; rep * to * once more and end k5 p5.

Row 5: K1, cable (hold behind), yo, k5, yo, cable (hold behind), *yo , k5, yo, cable (hold in front)*; rep * to * once more, end k1. The cables will cross in different directions.

Row 6: P5, *k7, p4*; rep * to * once more and end k7, p5 = 39 sts.

Rows 7–28: Continue working in garter st between the cables (every 6th row) and the yarnover increases on the RS so you increase a total of 6 sts on every other row.

Row 29 (5th cable crossing, RS): Change from garter st to moss st between the cables: yo, k1, *p1, k1*; rep * to

* to the next yarnover. On the WS, knit each yarnover and, between them, work knit over knit and purl over purl. See Chart B.

Row 35 (6th cable crossing): Return to garter st.

Row 59 (10th cable crossing): Moss st/UK double moss stitch.

Row 65 (11th cable crossing): Garter st.

Row 89 (15th cable crossing): Moss st/UK double moss stitch.

Row 95 (16th cable crossing): Garter st.

Work 1 more row = 309 sts.

BIND-OFF

This decorative bind-off is based on a multiple of 3 sts, so it doesn't matter if you've changed the shawl's size; the stitch count will work. The shawl begins with 21 sts, and because you increase a total of 6 sts on each increase row, the stitch count will always be a multiple of 3 sts.

RS: Join 3 knit sts with a centered double decrease (CDD)—slip 2 sts knitwise at the same time, k1, pass the slipped sts over knit st. *Place st back on left needle, k1 and slip off.** Rep * to ** 5 times (this sequence looks like crocheted chain sts).

Now work 1 CDD (see above) = 2 sts on right needle. Pass the right st over the left.*** Rep from * to *** until all the sts have been worked.

Cut yarn and draw end through last st.

FINISHING: Weave in all ends neatly on WS. Hand wash gently in lukewarm water and wool-safe soap. Block by pinning shawl out to finished measurements. Use blocking wires or pins to stretch out the loops along outer edges so that they look nice.

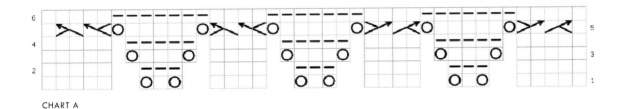

CHART A

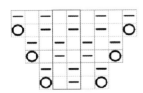

CHART B

PLAYFUL CHILDREN'S PONCHO

SKILL LEVEL INTERMEDIATE
SIZES 4-5 YEARS (8-9 YEARS)
FINISHED MEASUREMENTS
WIDTH: 17¾ (25½) IN / 45 (65) CM
LENGTH: 17¾ (23 ¾) IN / 45 (60) CM

MATERIALS
YARN:
CYCA #2 (SPORT) LANG NOVA (48% MERINO WOOL, 32% CAMEL, 20% NYLON, 197 YD/180 M / 25 G)
YARN AMOUNT AND COLOR:
5 (9) BALLS, COLOR 22
NEEDLES U.S. SIZE 10 / 6 MM: LONG CIRCULAR + 1 EXTRA NEEDLE FOR BIND-ING-OFF; SET OF 5 DPN OR 16 IN / 40 CM CIRCULAR FOR TURTLE NECK; CABLE NEEDLE
CROCHET HOOK U.S. SIZE H-8 / 5 MM
NOTIONS STITCH HOLDER; 5 BUTTONS
GAUGE
16 STS IN ST ST = 4 IN / 10 CM.
ADJUST NEEDLE SIZE TO OBTAIN COR-RECT GAUGE IF NECESSARY.

WHY MAKE A FUSS? A garment without a definite back or front is quite practical—both for the playful wearer and for the knitter. Finishing is minimal. The neck is shaped with short rows the same way on both pieces. You don't need to bind off, so you can work the totally simple turtleneck directly from the live stitches.

The cables, which cross in different directions, have sections of garter stitch and moss stitch/UK double moss stitch between them, making it easy to count the rows for the cable crossings. The edge stitches at the sides automatically fold under the wide cable for extra stability.

The shoulders are bound off and finished at the same time by using an extra needle, a nifty trick that yields lovely results.

PLAYFUL CHILDREN'S PONCHO

INFORMATION
Every row begins with sl 1 purlwise wyf. The second stitch is knitted, as are the last two stitches of each row. See Symbols Key on page 157.

FRONT AND BACK
CO 92 (132) sts.
Row 1 (WS): Sl 1 purlwise wyf, knit to end of row.
Row 2 (RS): Sl 1 purlwise, knit to end of row.
Row 3: Sl 1 purlwise, k1, *p8, k12*; rep * to * until 10 sts rem; end p8, k2.
Row 4: Sl 1 purlwise, k1, *k8, p2*; rep * to * until 10 sts rem and end k10.
Rep Rows 3-4 until you have worked 9 rows total.
Rows 10-29: Continue repeating Rows 3-4 and, *at the same time*, cross the cables following Chart A, B, A, B, A, (B, A, B, A, B, A, B) in the 5 (7) St st columns on Rows 10 and 20.
Row 30 and following: Continue crossing the cables following the charts on every 10th row and then work moss st/UK double moss stitch following Chart C instead of garter.

After 12 (15) cable crosses, it's time to begin shaping the neck. Turn as for the short row technique described on pages 136-137 to avoid stairsteps in your knitting.

Both sizes: With RS facing and following the chart, work 41 (61) sts; turn and work back.
Work 36 (56) sts; turn and work back.
Work 33 (53) sts; turn and work back.
Work 31 (51) sts; turn and work back.
Size 8-9 years only: Make another 3 short rows:
Work 49 sts; turn and work back.

Work 47 sts; turn and work back.
Work 45 sts; turn and work back.
Work the opposite side the same way but in reverse to correspond. *Do not* bind off. Instead, place rem sts on a holder; smooth cotton yarn or an extra needle will also work.
Make another piece the same way.

JOINING SHOULDERS
Place the two pieces with RS facing RS and, on both sides, work from the shoulder towards the neck.
BO 29 (44) sts on each piece with 3-needle bind-off (see page 134). *Do not* cut yarn or draw end through last st—instead, save both yarns to use for turtleneck (so the ribbing will be even and neat).

TURTLENECK
Place rem 70 (90) sts onto a U.S. 10 / 6 mm circular or divide onto 4 dpn. You should have 34 + 34 (44 + 44) sts + 1 st at each side from shoulder join. Begin at the front neck edge = 34 (44) sts. Work k1, *p2, k3*; rep from * to * until 2 sts rem and end k2. The center cable flows neatly into the ribbing (see photo below).

Work knit over knit and purl over purl until neck measures 6 (8) in / 15 (20) cm or desired length.

FINISHING
Cut yarn and weave in all ends neatly on WS. Gently wash poncho in lukewarm water with wool-safe soap. Block by patting out garment to finished measurements and leave until completely dry. If you want buttons on the poncho, securely sew 2 on each side. Crochet button loops with chain st centered on opposite side to match button placement.

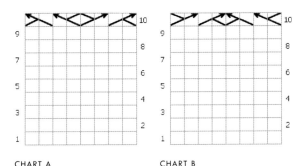

CHART A   CHART B

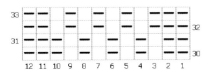

CHART C

THE RIBBING WILL LOOK DIFFERENT ON THE WRONG SIDE

APPEARANCES CAN DECEIVE SWEATER

SKILL LEVEL EXPERIENCED
SIZES S (M, L, XL)
FINISHED MEASUREMENTS
CHEST: 37 (41¼, 45¾, 50) IN / 94 (105, 116, 127) CM
LENGTH: 23 (24, 25, 26) IN / 58.5 (61, 63.5, 66) CM

MATERIALS
YARN:
CYCA #4 (WORSTED, AFGHAN, ARAN)
ÖSTERGÖTLANDS ULLSPINNERI RENEMO (100% WOOL, 219 YD/200 M / 100 G)
YARN AMOUNT AND COLOR:
6 (7, 7, 8) BALLS, WHITE
NEEDLES U.S. SIZES 4 AND 6 / 3.5 AND 4 MM: STRAIGHTS OR CIRCULAR

+ 1 EXTRA FOR BINDING-OFF; CABLE NEEDLE
NOTIONS STITCH HOLDER; STITCH MARKERS (OPTIONAL)
GAUGE
20 STS IN ST ST ON LARGER NEEDLES = 4 IN / 10 CM.
ADJUST NEEDLE SIZE TO OBTAIN CORRECT GAUGE IF NECESSARY.

THIS SWEATER IS EASIER TO KNIT than you might expect when you see the combination of cables and blocks. The pattern is easy partly because the cables are flanked by garter stitch columns, and partly because the stockinette (stocking stitch) blocks are the same width as the cable panels. For example, this way, you'll knit only knit stitches when the right side is facing. Narrow stockinette columns at the sides make it easy to finish neatly with mattress stitch (see page 135).

At the lower edge, garter stitch is combined with cables, which continue up the sweater, while the garter stitch is broken up by stockinette blocks. The first cable crossings occur on the second row and make a scalloped edge. If you want to avoid that effect, simply skip the first two rows and begin on Row 3.

APPEARANCES CAN DECEIVE SWEATER

BACK

With larger needles, CO 100 (112, 124, 136) sts (or use smaller needles for a firmer edge). The first row is worked on WS. Follow Chart A (B, A, B), working the repeat outlined in red for a total of 7 (9, 9, 11) cable columns. (See Symbols Key on page 157.) Work Rows 1-21.

If you started with smaller needles, change to larger needles; if you started with larger needles, continue. Rep Rows 22-29 (the garter st shifts to the St st block pattern) until there are 13 (13, 14, 14) St st blocks in length. End with Row 29.

Shape armholes at each side: BO the first 8 sts and complete row. BO the first 8 sts of next row; complete row and then CO 2 sts. Work next row, casting on 2 sts at end.

In order to have matching St st columns at the sides as before, work the first and last 4 sts as follows: With RS facing, sl 1 as est, k3 and k4 at end of row. With WS facing: sl 1, k1, p2 and work last 4 sts as p2, k2.

Continue repeating Rows 22-29 until back is 20 (21, 22, 23) blocks in length (end with Row 29). Shape neck with short rows (see pages 136-137) and as follows: With RS facing, work 35 (41, 41, 47) sts following the chart; turn and work back. Work 29 (35, 35, 41) sts; turn and work back. Work 23 (29, 29, 35) sts; turn and work back. The last row worked is Row 27 and the back now has 21 (22, 23, 24) blocks in length.

Do not cut yarn—you will knit with it eventually. Work the other side to correspond, using a new strand of yarn.

NOTE: Begin on WS, and work Row 22 and the following even-numbered rows as purl rows to end on a RS row. You don't want a yarn end at the center of the piece.

Knit 1 row across back with the first yarn end (in St st, it's better if you work each "wrap" together with the stitch it wraps around; but here, your stitches will wrap garter stitch, so you don't need to do that). *Do not* bind off. Instead, place sts on a holder; smooth cotton yarn or an extra needle will also work.

FRONT

Work as for back through armhole shaping. Continue by repeating Rows 22-29 until the front is 16 (17, 18, 19) blocks in length (end with Row 29).

With RS facing, shape neck: work following the chart through to the middle of the center cable. Turn; sl 2 sts purlwise wyf and continue following the chart. On RS, always knit the 2 sts for neck placket; on WS, slip those 2 sts.

Continue repeating Rows 22-29 until front is 19 (20, 21, 22) blocks in length (end with Row 29). Shape front neck with short rows as follows: Work following chart until 9 (9, 15, 15) sts rem to placket; turn as for back. On the next short row, turn when 15 (15, 21, 21) sts rem, then 18 (18, 24, 24) sts, and finally 21 (21, 27, 27) sts. Continue straight up until front is 21 (22, 23, 24) blocks in length, ending with Row 27 on chart.

With RS facing, knit 1 row and, *at the same time*, pick up and knit about 5 sts along the garter st straight edge.

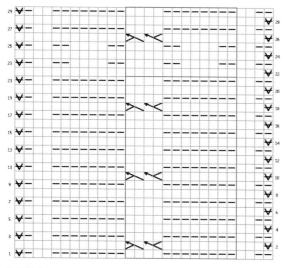

CHART A

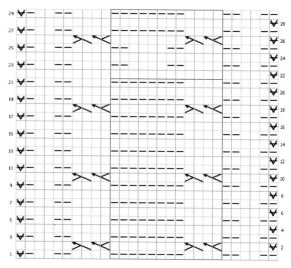

CHART B

INSTEAD OF HIDING THE SHOULDER SEAM, WHY NOT EMPHASIZE IT FOR EFFECT?

Even here, you can let the "wraps" remain because they won't be visible.

Work the other side of the placket the same way but reversed to correspond.

NOTE: Begin on WS as for back and purl Row 22 and all following even-numbered rows.

JOINING SHOULDERS
Place the front and back pieces with right sides facing *out* to join the two sets of 23 (29, 29, 35) shoulder sts. Three-needle bind-off with the right sides facing out makes a distinctive edge on the RS (see photo above), which I think goes well with the overall pattern. Use an extra needle to k2tog with the first st from each needle; *join next st on each needle with k2tog and then pass st at right on right needle over left st (see page 134). Continue the same way from * until all the shoulder sts have been joined. Cut yarn and draw end through last st. You now have an edge that folds easily. If you want to have a matching edge on both shoulders, work towards the center on one shoulder and out from the center on the other shoulder.

I-CORD
Begin with the first cord that will hang on the front. With smaller dpn, CO 3 sts. Knit across and then slide sts back to front of left needle; knit across, pulling yarn across back of work. Continue until cord is desired length (for example, 50 rows). Now knit together with the sts along neck edge (see photo on next page).

Place all the sts of neck edge on a circular. K2 (cord), k2tog tbl (one st from cord with one from neck edge), and slide the sts onto left needle. Continue the same way until you've worked all around the neck and then knit a matching length cord the same way as at the beginning, but use the 3 sts remaining after the last join with the neck edge. End with k3tog; cut yarn and draw end through last loop.

SLEEVES (MAKE BEFORE SEAMING SIDES)
Alternative 1: Pick up and knit sts directly on the sweater. CO 2 sts for the edge sts and then pick up and knit 96 (108, 108, 120) sts between the garter st edge and the St st column (see pages 38-39), skipping every 4th row. Make sure that there are the same number of sts on each side of the center so the pattern is centered. End by cast-

ing on 2 edge sts = 100 (112, 112, 124) sts total.
Alternative 2: *Work the sleeves separately, from top down.*
CO 100 (112, 112, 124) sts and work a couple of rows before beginning the pattern so there will be a seam allowance for finishing.

BOTH ALTERNATIVES

Follow Chart A (B, B, A) working the repeat so there are 7 (9, 9, 9) cable columns.

NOTE: The first row is Row 19, which is worked from the WS. The 4 center sts are for a cable. The outermost 4 sts at each side are worked as for the front and back edge sts.

The first decrease is made at the same time as the first cable crossing (Row 26 on the chart). K2tog with sts 4 and 5 by slipping them knitwise one at a time. Place sts back on needle and then knit tog tbl (left-leaning decrease) = ssk. Work until 5 sts rem and then k2tog (right-leaning decrease), k3.

Decrease the same way on every 6th row until about 2½ in / 6 cm rem to desired total sleeve length. When you reach the elbow, compare the sleeve with those on a sweater you feel comfortable in. You might want to change to more or fewer rows between decreases for the second half of the sleeve. Finish the sleeve with garter st between the cable columns for about 2½ in / 6 cm so the cuffs match the lower edge of the sweater. BO.

FINISHING

It's easiest to begin by attaching the sleeves, if you didn't pick up sts directly around the armhole. Begin at the center (shoulder seam) so the cables will match along the shoulder line.

Seam the sides with mattress stitch (see page 135), either all the way down to lower edge or leaving the garter section of the edge open for a split hem. Seam sleeves with mattress stitch. Weave in all ends neatly on WS.

Gently wash sweater in lukewarm water with wool-safe soap. Block by patting or pinning out garment to finished measurements; leave until completely dry.

KNIT AN I-CORD TOGETHER WITH STITCHES PICKED UP AT NECK (YARN: MALABRIGO RIOS, COLOR: REFLECTING POOL)

SWEATER HISTORY

SKILL LEVEL EXPERIENCED
SIZES S (M, L)
FINISHED MEASUREMENTS
CHEST: 35½ (41, 46½) IN / 90 (104, 118) CM
LENGTH: 21¼ (22, 22¾) IN / 54 (56, 58) CM
MATERIALS
YARN:
CYCA #4 (WORSTED, AFGHAN, ARAN)

CASCADE YARNS CASCADE 220 (100% PERUVIAN HIGHLAND WOOL, 220 YD/201 M / 100 G)
YARN AMOUNT AND COLOR:
5 (6, 7) SKEINS, COLOR HEATHERS 9449 (9488)
NEEDLES U.S. SIZE 6 / 4 MM: STRAIGHTS OR CIRCULAR + 1 EXTRA FOR BINDING OFF;
U.S. SIZE 4 / 3.5 MM: 16 IN / 40 CM

CIRCULAR FOR NECKBAND; CABLE NEEDLE
NOTIONS STITCH HOLDER; STITCH MARKERS (OPTIONAL)
GAUGE
20 STS IN ST ST ON LARGER NEEDLES = 4 IN / 10 CM.
ADJUST NEEDLE SIZES TO OBTAIN CORRECT GAUGE IF NECESSARY.

HOW THE YEARS FLY! I knitted the first version of this sweater in 2006 for my colleague Karin in Örebro, where I lived for a few years. My idea then was to create a timeless garment with a sense of history—something that would suit a history teacher. Those considerations led to this combination of lattice patterns, moss stitch/UK double moss stitch, and stockinette (stocking stitch) columns, with a split hem at each side and a square neckline. Later, I knitted similar garments with different variations, but for me it is still "Karin's sweater."

This would be a good project for anyone who wants to work with various cable patterns on the same row. The cables cross on every eighth row in the narrow columns, so they'll land at the same crossing rows as in the large lattice pattern. That approach makes it easier to knit and also enhances the overall impression.

SWEATER HISTORY

The lattice pattern in the center is the same for all sizes, with the width adjusted by changing the number of moss stitches in the side columns. The cables on the front and back edges are mirror images of each other, which forms a new pattern when you seam the pieces (see photo to right). The same pattern also appears on the sleeves. The garter stitch lower edges don't distract from the cable patterns, and they're easy to knit—or easy to change, if you like. Perhaps you'd rather substitute ribbing or moss stitch/UK double moss stitch?

Size S corresponds approximately to children's size 10-12 years. For that size, the sleeve shaping is made more often, on about every fourth row.

INFORMATION

Edge Sts (not shown on chart): Always slip the first st purlwise wyf on all rows. Always knit the second st of row as well as the last two sts.

NOTE: Chart A is on the right side of the page because you knit from right to left.

FRONT

With larger needles, CO 93 (107, 121) sts. Knit 7 (11, 15) rows garter st (the first and last rows = WS).

With RS facing, begin and end rows with edge sts. Work following Chart A: Sts 1-25 (1-25 + 19-25, 1-25 + 12-25). See Symbols Key on page 137. Work following Chart B (the same for all sizes). Next, work Chart C: Sts 1-25 (1-7 + 1-25, 1-14 + 1-25) = 100 (114, 128) sts total.

NOTE: To avoid holes from the yarnover increases, work yarnovers as p1tbl on following row.

Work edge sts as est. Repeat Rows 11-18 on Charts A and C and Rows 3-18 on Chart B. When piece measures 12¾ (13, 13½) in / 32 (33, 34) cm, BO 8 (8, 8) sts each at beginning of next two rows for armhole shaping = 84 (98, 112) sts rem.

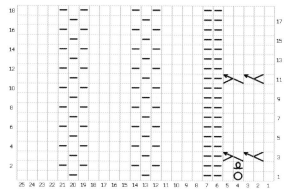

CHART C

CHART A

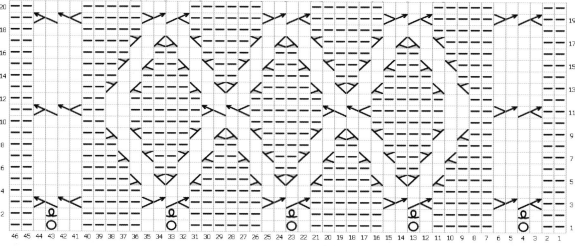

CHART B

THE CABLES AT THE OUTER EDGES FORM A NEW PATTERN ONCE SEAMED

If you would like the St st columns at the sides to have the same width, you can cast on 2 new sts for edge sts. Continue to work following the charts and to work the edge sts as est.

End Chart B after completing 8 (8, 8) repeats and divide for neck. Change the outermost cables at the sides of Chart B to St st. Place the center 34 sts on a holder for neck. CO 1 extra st at neck edge and always knit that st on all rows. Work straight up until piece measures 21¼ (22, 22¾) in / 54 (56, 58) cm.
Do not bind off. Instead, place sts on a holder; smooth cotton yarn or an extra needle will also work. Work the other side to correspond.

BACK
Work back as for front but with 8 extra rows before placing the center 34 sts on a holder for back neck. See Chart E for a suggestion about how to finish the lattice pattern. Work each side straight up as for front (with an extra st at neck edge on each side) until the front and back pieces are the same length.

JOINING SHOULDERS
Join the back and front at each shoulder with three-needle bind-off. With RS facing RS (so WS is facing out), use an extra needle to k2tog with the first st from each needle; *join next st on each needle with k2tog and then pass st at right on right needle over left st (see page 134). Continue the same way from * until all the shoulder sts have been joined. Cut yarn and draw end through last st. Join the second shoulder the same way.

SLEEVES (MAKE BOTH ALIKE)
With RS facing and beginning at center of underarm, CO 2 sts and pick up and knit about 88 (92, 96) sts inside edge sts, making sure you pick up the same number of sts on each side of armhole (see pages 38-39). The exact number is not that important here. End by casting on 2 sts.
NOTE: The two extra sts at each side are edge sts and worked as for edge sts on front and back.

Purl 1 row (= WS). Pm around the center 52 (66, 66) sts or 26 (33, 33) sts on each side of shoulder seam. Work in St st up to first marker.

Begin with Chart D: Work sts 1-7 2 (3, 3) times = 14 (21, 21) sts, work sts 8-31 once (all sizes) = 24 sts and then work sts 32-38 2 (3, 3) times = 14 (21, 21) sts.

End the row in St st plus the two edge sts. Work through Row 10 the same way.

The sleeve shaping begins on Row 11, with the decreases then repeated on every 8th row (on the same row as the cable crossings). Try on the sleeve occasionally to decide if you need to adjust the number of rows between decreases. (You might need to work them as often as every 4th row on the smallest size).

Decreases: K2tog with the 4th and 5th sts at beginning of row as follows: Sl 1 purlwise, k2, ssk. Continue following the chart until 5 sts rem, k2tog, and then knit rem sts. Continue decreases and charted rows as est until sleeve is desired length.

Finish with garter st as for the lower edge of the front. BO. Leave enough yarn (about 1½ times the sleeve length) for sewing the sleeve seam so you'll have fewer ends to weave in later on.

NECKBAND
Place the saved sts of back neck onto circular U.S. size 4 / 3.5 mm and knit the sts; yo, pick up and knit approx. 22 (24, 26) sts inside edge sts, yo, work 34 sts of front neck, yo, pick up and knit the same number of sts along the other edge, and end with yo. The 4 yarnovers form the corners of the neckband; mark each corner. Join to work around.

Rnd 1: K1, purl until 1 st rem before first yo, *k1, k1tbl (into yarnover), k1, purl until 1 st before next yo*. Rep * to * until 1 st (= yo rem, k1tbl into yarnover.

Rnd 2: Knit to the 3 knit sts in first corner. *CDD (sl 2 sts knitwise at same time, k1, psso). Knit to next set of 3 knit sts at corner*. Rep * to * until 2 sts rem on rnd. CDD as before (one of the sts is first st of rnd).

Rnd 3: K1, *purl until 1 st rem before decrease, k3*. Rep * to * until 2 sts rem, k2.

Rep Rnds 2-3 once more or until band is desired height (don't forget about size of neck opening as you eliminate 8 sts on every decrease rnd). End with Rnd 2. BO.

FINISHING
Join the side seams with mattress st (see page 135), working in the St st inside the edge sts. Seam the entire length or leave a split hem open at bottom edge. Seam sleeves with mattress stitch. Weave in all ends neatly on WS. Gently wash sweater in lukewarm water with wool-safe soap. Block by patting or pinning out garment to finished measurements; leave until completely dry.

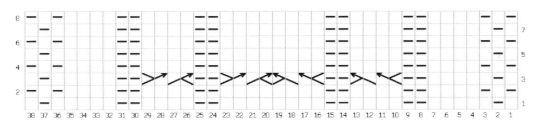

CHART D

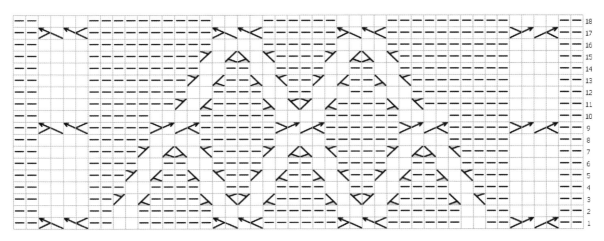

CHART E

CROSSWISE VEST

SKILL LEVEL EXPERIENCED
SIZES S (M, L, XL)
FINISHED MEASUREMENTS
CHEST: 34¾ (37¾, 41, 44) IN / 88 (96, 104, 112) CM
LENGTH: 22 (22¾, 23¾, 24½) IN / 56 (58, 60, 62) CM

MATERIALS
YARN:
CYCA #5 (BULKY) SANDNES FRITIDS-GARN (100% WOOL, 77 YD/70 M / 50 G)
YARN AMOUNT AND COLOR:
7 (8, 9, 10) SKEINS, COLOR 2641 NAT-URAL HEATHER
NEEDLES U.S. SIZE 8 / 5 MM: STRAIGHTS OR CIRCULAR + 1 EXTRA

FOR BINDING OFF;
U.S. SIZE 7 / 4.5 MM: 16 IN / 40 CM CIRCULAR FOR NECKBAND; CABLE NEEDLE
NOTIONS STITCH HOLDER; STITCH MARKERS
GAUGE
15 STS IN ST ST ON LARGER NEEDLES = 4 IN / 10 CM.
ADJUST NEEDLE SIZE TO OBTAIN COR-RECT GAUGE IF NECESSARY.

A VEST is a comfortable garment that's also warm. Vests are a good project for anyone who wants to try a larger project but doesn't want to knit and finish an entire sweater or cardigan. This vest has minimal finishing—the shoulders are joined with three-needle bind-off and only the sides need to be seamed. The I-cord around the neck is easy to make and doesn't require any special stitch count.

If you're being precise, this pattern uses traveling stitches rather than cables, but the principle is the same: Stitches change places before being knitted. Throughout, it's just a question of a knit and a purl stitch. The pattern repeat is small and easy to memorize. It's repeated over a large surface for a rich effect.

CROSSWISE VEST

BACK

With U.S. 8 / 5 mm needles, CO 77 (83, 89, 95) sts. The two outermost sts at each side are edge sts; St st columns (2 sts wide) are inside the edge sts.

Row 1 (WS): Sl 1 purlwise, k1, p2, knit until 4 sts rem, p2, k2.

Row 2 (RS): Sl 1 purlwise, knit to end of row.

Row 3 (see chart A): Sl 1 purlwise, k1, p2, k3, *p3, k3*; rep * to * until 4 sts rem, end p2, k2.

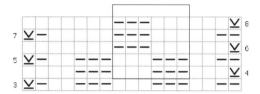

CHART A

See Symbols Key on page 157. Continue working block pattern on Chart A until you have 3 (3, 5, 5) blocks in length.

On next RS row: Work edge sts and in block pattern as est over 13 (16, 19, 22) sts, k51 (= row 1 of chart B); end with block pattern and edge sts over rem 13 (16, 19, 22) sts.

Continue working edge sts and block pattern at the sides and Chart B over the center 51 sts. On Chart B, repeat Rows 4–23.

Now there are 25 (27, 27, 29) blocks in length at the sides = approx. 12¾ (13½, 13½, 14¼) in / 32 (34, 34, 36) cm and it's time to decrease at the sides to shape armholes and cast on new edge sts.

On next RS row: BO the first 7 (7, 7, 7) sts, k1, p1, continue charted pattern to end of row.

On next WS row: BO the first 7 (7, 7, 7) sts, p1, k1, work in charted pattern until 3 sts rem, k1, p2, and end by casting on 2 new edge sts.

On next RS row: Sl 1 purlwise, k3, p1, work following chart until 3 sts rem, p1, k2, CO 2 new edge sts = 67 (73, 79, 85) sts.

At each side, there are 2 edge sts and 2 St st columns, as before, as well as a purl column inside them. The 1 (2, 3, 4) blocks are framed by purl columns.

Continue working following the chart until piece measures approx. 20½ (21¼, 22, 22¾) in / 52 (54, 56, 58) cm and then begin shaping neck with short rows (see pages 136–137). The piece will look best if you end on an iteration of Row 4, 12, 14, or 22 of Chart B, because you complete a pattern on those rows. Mark your ending row on the chart so later you can easily choose the corresponding row number of a pattern repeat further down on the front.

Begin short rows:

On RS: Pm around the center 19 (19, 19, 19) sts and work to first marker; turn (see pages 136–137) and work to end of row following chart.

Following short rows: Turn 3 sts before the first turn, and then 2 sts, and, finally, 2 sts = 17 (20, 23, 26) sts.

Do not bind off. Instead, place rem st on a holder; smooth cotton yarn or an extra needle will also work.

Work the other side to correspond, mirror-imaging short row shaping.

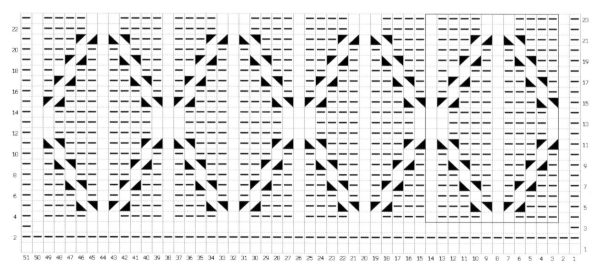

CHART B

THE I-CORD AROUND THE NECKLINE MAKES A NICE EDGING

FRONT

Work as for back until piece measures 17¾ (18½, 19¼, 20) in / 45 (47, 49, 51) cm. End with the same row in pattern as for back neck but 1 pattern rep (20 rows) earlier.

Pm around the center 9 (9, 9, 9) sts. Work short rows as for back neck, turning at marker for first time, and then 3-3-2-2-2 sts before previous turn. After completing short row shaping, work straight up until front is same length as back. *Do not* bind off but place sts on a holder. Work the other side to correspond, mirror-imaging short row shaping.

JOINING SHOULDERS

Place back and front with RS facing RS and join with 3-needle bind-off. Use an extra needle to k2tog with the first st from each needle; *join next st on each needle with k2tog and then pass st at right on right needle over left st (see page 134). Continue the same way from * until all the shoulder sts have been joined. Cut yarn and draw end through last st.

NECKBAND

Slip all the live sts on holders to a circular smaller cir-cular. Begin at center back or at a shoulder (there will be a small seam, so it's good to try to place this where it will be least visible). Begin by knitting 1 row around the neck edge, *at the same time* picking up and knitting about 3 sts for every 4 rows along the straight edges from shoulders. Preferably with a knitted CO, CO new sts: *K1 *but* do not slip it off left needle, k1 into previous st and place new st back on left needle*; rep * to * until there are 3 new sts.

Now make an I-cord (see photo on page 84): K2 and then k2tog tbl (joining st of cord with one from neck edge). *Slip sts back to left needle, k2, k2tog tbl (with one st each from I-cord and neck*). Rep * to * around. Sew the rem 3 sts to CO edge of cord.

FINISHING

Seam the sides with mattress st (see page 135); work all the way to bottom edges or leave a split hem, whichever you prefer. The edge sts around the armholes will auto-matically roll inwards, but you can tack them down if you wish. Weave in all ends neatly on WS. Gently wash vest in lukewarm water with wool-safe soap. Block by patting or pinning out garment to finished measurements; leave until completely dry.

FREE AND EASY TOP

SKILL LEVEL EXPERIENCED
SIZES XS (S, M, L)
FINISHED MEASUREMENTS
CHEST: 39½ (41, 42½, 44) IN / 100 (104, 108, 112) CM
LENGTH: 21¼ (22, 22¾, 23¾) IN / 54 (56, 58, 60) CM

MATERIALS
YARN:
CYCA #1 (FINGERING) GEILSK 3-PLY BOMULD OG ULD (COTTON AND WOOL) (55% WOOL, 45% COTTON, 254 YD/232 M / 50 G)
YARN AMOUNT AND COLOR:
4 (4, 5, 5) BALLS, COLOR 25
NEEDLES U.S. SIZE 6 / 4 MM: 2 32 IN / 80 CM CIRCULARS + 1 EXTRA FOR BINDING OFF;
U.S. SIZE 4 / 3.5 MM: 16 OR 24 IN / 40 OR 60 CM CIRCULAR FOR NECKBAND; CABLE NEEDLE
NOTIONS STITCH MARKERS
GAUGE
21 STS IN ST ST ON LARGER NEEDLES = 4 IN / 10 CM.
ADJUST NEEDLE SIZE TO OBTAIN CORRECT GAUGE IF NECESSARY.

EARLY ON, A BOOK ABOUT FISHERMEN'S SWEATERS on Grandmother's bookshelf gave me a good introduction to Guernsey sweaters and their cable and texture patterns. The inspiration for this top comes right out of that knitting tradition, even if this is a very different style of garment. The wide short sleeves and relatively loose knitting, in a blend of wool and cotton, makes this top much better for relaxing than working long days at sea.

The top is worked in the round to the underarms. The moss stitch/UK double moss stitch at the sides makes it easier to see when it's time to cross the cables. You'll cast on new stitches for the sleeves, which are worked at the same time as the front and back pieces. That makes for a fine drape and minimal finishing.

FREE AND EASY TOP

LOWER EDGES, FRONT AND BACK

With larger circular, CO 233 (241, 249, 257) sts. Join, being careful not to twist cast-on row. Pm for beginning of rnd. Purl 1 rnd.

Work around in k2, p2 ribbing for 14 (14, 16, 16) rnds (see Chart A and the Symbols Key on page 157). Because you're working with an odd number of stitches, the ribbing spirals around. Make sure to move the beginning of rnd marker up every rnd to keep your place.

Purl 1 rnd. Now increase 1 st between last and first st of rnd (= a new last st of rnd). Purl 1 rnd = 234 (242, 250 258) sts.

Now work in pattern following charts:

B over 12 sts = left side chain cable.

C over 14 (16, 18, 20) sts as follows: 1-12 + 19-20. (1-14 + 19-20; 1-16 + 19-20; 1-20).

D over 8 sts, E over 15 sts, D over 8 sts, E over 15 sts, D over 8 sts, E over 15 sts, D over 8 sts.

C over 14 (16, 18, 20) sts as above.

Rep the chart sequence for the right side chain cable and back.

Continue, working charted patterns as est. When piece measures 13½ (13¾, 13¾, 14¼) in / 34 (35, 35, 36) cm, read NOTE before continuing.

NOTE: *Do not* work the last 2 sts of rnd so you can work an even number of sts for Chart D and can continue crossing the cables with RS facing you. The next step is to divide the work for front and back.

Row 1: Work 1 row following the charts as est and, *at the same time,* BO 16 sts at each side = BO 12 sts on Chart B as well as the k2 sts on each side of that. Begin all the bind-offs with the last 2 unworked sts of previous row. End the row by casting on (using knitted cast-on as for neck described at end of instructions) 10 (10, 12, 12) sts for the sleeve. Now work the back on a new circular, back and forth; leave front sts resting on the other circular.

Row 2 (WS): Purl the new sts to make finishing easier. Work following the charts as before and end row by casting 10 (10, 12, 12) sts for the sleeve.

Row 3: Knit the new sts. At end of row, continue in moss st/UK double moss stitch and end by casting on 8 (10, 10, 10) sts.

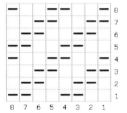

CHART A

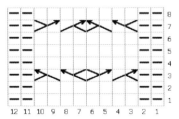

CHART B

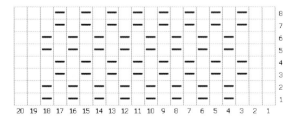

CHART C

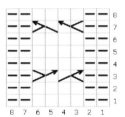

CHART D

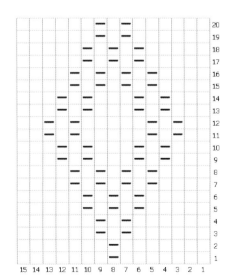

CHART E

Row 4: Purl the new sts and then work following charts and in moss st/UK double moss st as est. End by casting on 8 (10, 10, 10) sts.

Row 5: Knit the new sts and then work following charts and in moss st/UK double moss st as est. End by casting on 8 (8, 8, 10) sts.

Row 6: Purl the new sts and then work as est. End by casting on 8 (8, 8, 10) sts.

Row 7: Knit the new sts and then work as est. End by casting on 8 (8, 8, 8) sts.

Row 8: Purl the new sts and then work as est. End by casting on 8 (8, 8, 8) sts = 169 (177, 185, 193) sts.

Row 9: Knit the new sts and then work in pattern until 8 sts rem. End k2, p2, k4.

Row 10: P4, k2, p2 and then continue in pattern until 8 sts rem. End p2, k2, p4.

Row 11 (RS): Work following Chart F; continue in pattern until 8 sts rem and work following Chart G. Continue as est until piece measures 19¾ (20½, 21¼, 22) in / 50 (52, 54, 56) cm, ending with a WS row.

Work the outermost 8 sts at each side as before following Charts F and G and, between them, 2 rows reverse St st (purl on RS and knit on WS).

Work the front the same way.

BACK NECK SHAPING

The neckline is shaped with short rows (see pages 136-137). Turn on every other row with 3 sts between turns each time.

Rows 1-6: Continue working outermost 8 sts at each side as before (Charts F and G), and, between them, Chart A.

Row 7: Work 64 (68, 71, 75) sts; turn and work Row 8.

Row 9: Work 61 (65, 68, 72) sts; turn and work Row 10.

Row 11: Work 58 (62, 65, 69) sts; turn and work Row 12.

Do *not* bind off but place sts on a holder. Work the other side to correspond, reversing shaping. Do *not* bind off.

FRONT NECK SHAPING

Row 1: Work the first 8 sts as est (following Chart F) and then Chart A until you've worked a total of 73 (77, 80, 84) sts. Turn and work Row 2.

Row 3: Work 70 (74, 77, 81) sts; turn and work Row 4.

Row 5: Work 67 (71, 74, 78) sts; turn and work Row 6.

Row 7: Work 64 (68, 71, 75) sts; turn and work Row 8.

Row 9: Work 61 (65, 68, 72) sts; turn and work Row 10.

Row 11: Work 58 (62, 65, 69) sts; turn and work Row 12.

Do *not* bind off but place sts on a holder. Work the other side to correspond, reversing shaping. Do *not* bind off.

JOINING SHOULDERS

The front and back pieces are joined with right sides facing out, so there will be a decorative ridge along each shoulder from sleeve to neck.

Place back and front with WS facing WS and join with 3-needle bind-off. Use an extra needle to k2tog with the first st from each needle; *join next st on each needle with k2tog and then pass st at right on right needle over left st (see page 134). Continue the same way from * until all 58 (62, 65, 69) sts have been bound off at each shoulder. Cut yarn *but* do not draw end through last st. Save last st for the neck edging. Do *not* cut yarn after joining opposite shoulder so you can use it for neck edging.

NECK EDGING

Slip sts around the neck to smaller circular and knit 1 row. CO 3 sts with knitted CO:* k1, leaving st on left needle*; rep * to * until you have 3 new sts.

Now make an I-cord (see photo on page 84): K2 and then k2tog tbl (joining st of cord with one st of neck edge). *Slip sts back to left needle, k2, k2tog tbl (with one st each from I-cord and neck*). Rep * to * across. Sew the rem 3 sts to CO edge of cord.

FINISHING

Seam sleeves. Weave in all ends neatly on WS. Gently wash top in lukewarm water with wool-safe soap. Block by patting or pinning out garment to finished measurements; leave until completely dry.

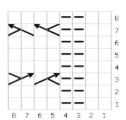

CHART G

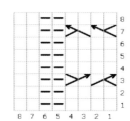

CHART F

FIGURE EIGHTS VEST

SKILL LEVEL EXPERIENCED
SIZES S (M, L)
FINISHED MEASUREMENTS
CHEST: 36¼ (39¾, 43¼) IN / 92 (101, 110) CM
LENGTH: 22½ (24½, 26½) IN / 57 (62, 67) CM

MATERIALS
YARN:
CYCA #4 (WORSTED, AFGHAN, ARAN)
ÖSTERGÖTLANDS ULLSPINNERI RENEMO
(100% WOOL, 219 YD/200 M / 100 G)
YARN AMOUNT AND COLOR:
4 (4, 5) BALLS, WHITE
NEEDLES U.S. SIZE 6 / 4 MM: 2 32 IN /
80 CM CIRCULARS OR 1 CIRCULAR AND

PAIR OF STRAIGHTS + 1 EXTRA FOR
BINDING-OFF; U.S. SIZE 4 / 3.5 MM: 16
IN / 40 CM CIRCULAR; CABLE NEEDLE
NOTIONS STITCH MARKERS (OPTIONAL)
GAUGE
20 STS IN ST ST ON LARGER NEEDLES =
4 IN / 10 CM.
ADJUST NEEDLE SIZE TO OBTAIN COR-
RECT GAUGE IF NECESSARY.

CABLE PATTERNS on a stockinette (stocking stitch) background produce a special effect, but it can be a little difficult to see where you are in the pattern because of the freestanding shapes with no other patterns to set them off. For that reason, I recommend you place markers between the repeats.

This is a good garment choice for anyone only moderately fond of finishing. The body is worked in the round to the armholes and the shoulders are joined with three-needle bind-off, so there are no seams to sew. The neckband, which doesn't need a precise number of stitches, rolls into shape and is very easy to knit.

FIGURE EIGHTS VEST

Depending on the size, different parts of the pattern land on center front. If you are working size S, the half figure is centered; for size M, the area between the half and whole figure eight is at the center; and for size L, a whole figure eight. If you want to rearrange the symmetry, I've added suggestions for adjusting the patterns to the instructions.

BACK AND FRONT
With larger circular, CO 200 (220, 240) sts; join, being careful not to twist cast-on row. Pm for beginning of rnd.

Work following the chart (see Symbols Key on page 157), repeating the 20 sts 10 (11, 12) times around. First work Rows 1-48 and then rep Rows 21-48 until piece measures 13½ (14½, 15¾) in / 34 (37, 40) cm. End with an even-numbered row so the cable crosses can continue on the RS.

NOTE: If you decide to shift the pattern arrangement by reversing some of the stitches, one alternative is to work a bit into the next row in order to change the motif at center front (see below).

SHIFTING THE PATTERN PLACEMENT

If you want to adjust the pattern placement, the placement of the armholes must also be changed. In that case, decide what you want at center front (the dividing line between 2 sts) and count 54 (59, 64) sts to the right. Then you can begin binding off 8 sts as described below.

DIVIDE BODY FOR FRONT AND BACK
BO 8 sts, work 92 (102, 112) sts following chart, BO 8 sts and work 92 (102, 112) sts following chart. Turn piece and place back sts on a second circular; leave front sts on first circular.

Shape armholes by binding off 2-2-2 (3-2-2; 3-3-2) sts at beginning of the following 6 rows; otherwise, continue in charted pattern = 80 (88, 96) sts rem.

Work in pattern until piece measures 21¾ (23¾, 25½) in / 55 (60, 65) cm.

NOTE: The neckline is shaped over the last 6 rows, so I recommend you take note of where you are on the chart. Perhaps you would prefer to work in stockinette (stocking stitch) instead of beginning a new cable pattern that won't affect the finishing? (See the knitted sample in the photos, where I allowed the figure-eight rings nearest the front neckline to be half-eights.)

On RS: Work 30 (33, 36) sts. Turn, BO 3 sts and complete row. BO 3 sts at neck edge on every other row another 2 times = 21 (24, 27) sts rem. *Do not* bind off.

Shape the other side the same way, reversing shaping to correspond.

FRONT
Shape armholes as for back and then work straight up following the chart until piece measures 19¾ (21¾, 23¾) in / 50 (55, 60) cm. Shape neckline beginning on RS: Work 33 (36, 39) sts. Turn, BO 3 sts and complete row. Continue binding off at neck edge on every other row: 3-2-2-2 sts = 21 (24, 27) sts rem. Continue without further shaping until piece is same length as back. *Do not* bind off.

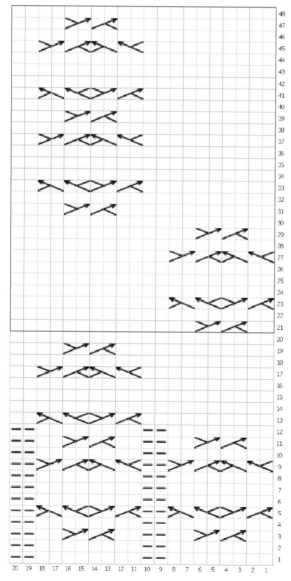

CHART

THE CABLE PATTERN DRAWS IN THE ADJOINING STITCHES SLIGHTLY.

Shape other side of front neck the same way, reversing shaping to correspond. Leave the sts on the needle to that you can join the front and back with 3-needle BO.

JOINING SHOULDERS

Place back and front with RS facing RS and join with 3-needle bind-off. Use an extra needle to k2tog with the first st from each needle; *join next st on each needle with k2tog and then pass st at right on right needle over left st (see page 134). Continue the same way from * until all 21 (24, 27) sts have been bound off at each shoulder. Cut yarn and draw end through last st. Join the other shoulder the same way.

NECK EDGING

With RS facing and smaller circular: Beginning at one shoulder seam, pick up and knit 2 sts for every 3 rows on straight edges and 1 st for each bound-off st around neckline; also knit the rem 14 (16, 18 front neck and 20 (22, 24) sts of back neck as you work around.

Turn work inside out and. Knit 8 rnds for an edge that rolls inwards. There will be a little gap at the turn but you can sew it closed when you weave in the yarn ends. BO loosely so the edge doesn't draw in.

ARMHOLE EDGING

With RS facing and smaller circular: Beginning at center of underarm, pick up and knit 3 sts for every 4 rows around. Pick up a multiple of 4 sts—if necessary, you can increase or decrease on the first round to adjust the total.

Work 6 rnds in k2, p2 ribbing. BO in ribbing.

FINISHING

Weave in all ends neatly on WS. Gently wash vest in lukewarm water with wool-safe soap. Block by patting or pinning out garment to finished measurements; leave until completely dry.

X & O CARDIGAN

SKILL LEVEL EXPERIENCED
SIZES S (M, L)
FINISHED MEASUREMENTS
CHEST: 37¾ (41, 44) IN / 96 (104, 112) CM
LENGTH: 26¾ (27½, 28¼) IN / 68 (70, 72) CM

MATERIALS
YARN:
CYCA #4 (WORSTED, AFGHAN, ARAN)
ÖSTERGÖTLANDS ULLSPINNERI RENEMO
(100% WOOL, 219 YD/200 M / 100 G)
YARN AMOUNT AND COLOR:
7 (8, 8) SKEINS, RED
NEEDLES U.S. SIZE 6 / 4 MM:
STRAIGHTS OR CIRCULAR + 1 EXTRA
FOR BINDING-OFF;

U.S. SIZE 4 / 3.5 MM: 32 IN / 80 CM
CIRCULAR FOR RIBBED EDGES; CABLE
NEEDLE
NOTIONS STITCH HOLDER; STITCH
MARKERS; APPROX. 6 BUTTONS
GAUGE
20 STS IN ST ST ON U.S. SIZE 4 / 6 MM
NEEDLES = 4 IN / 10 CM.
ADJUST NEEDLE SIZE TO OBTAIN COR-
RECT GAUGE IF NECESSARY.

THE X AND O CABLE PATTERN is one of my favorites, so I absolutely had to include a garment with it in the book. I envisioned a cardigan with only that cable motif cascading down its entire length, to show it off in its full glory.

In between the cables, I added a textured knit and purl design of diagonal lines. Stockinette (stocking stitch) and garter stitch columns frame the edges, while k3, p2 ribbing flows naturally into the other motifs. The same ribbing appears on the button and buttonhole bands, which join at the back neck.

The silhouette is straight, so the length is easy to adjust to suit your own preferences—but don't forget that changes in the length mean adjustments to the yarn amounts (and maybe an additional button).

X & O CARDIGAN

BACK

With smaller circular, CO 110 (120, 130) sts.

Row 1 (WS): Sl 1 purlwise, k1 (= edge sts), p2, k2, (p3, k2) until 4 sts rem; end p2, k2 (= edge sts).

Row 2: Sl 1 purlwise, (k3, p2) until 4 sts rem; end k4.
Rep these 2 rows until you've worked 13 (15, 17) rows total.

Change to larger circular and begin pattern on RS. Pm two markers as indicated below to make it easier to see where you are in the pattern, at least until the diagonal pattern begins to show clearly.

Row 1: Sl 1 purlwise, k8 (13, 18), pm, work following Charts A, B, A, C, A, B, A, C, A, pm, knit to end of row. For charts, see Symbols Key on page 157.

Row 2: Sl 1 purlwise, k1, p2, (k2, p3) to marker, work pattern following Charts A, C, A, B, A, C, A, B, A to next marker. Work (p3, k2) until 4 sts rem; end p2, k2.

Rep Rows 1-2 until back measures 17¼ (17¾, 18¼) in / 44 (45, 46) cm. Pm at each side to indicate beginning of armhole so you can match the rows on the front later on.

Shape armholes:

Row 1: BO 7 sts; complete row as est.

Row 2: BO 7 sts; complete row as est, CO 2 sts at end of row. Work new sts on Rows 2-2 as edge sts.

Row 3: Work row as est and then CO 2 sts at end of row = 100 (110, 120) sts.

When back measures approx. 24½ (25½, 26½)

in / 62 (65, 67) cm, shape back neck with short rows (see pages 136-137). Begin on a cable-crossing row so the piece will meet nicely at the shoulder seams. If you begin on Row 1 or 13 of Chart A, a circle will form at the shoulder seam; with Row 5 or 9 on Chart A, a cross forms.

With RS facing, work 40 (45, 50) sts (including edge sts); turn for short row and work in pattern to end of row.

Work 36 (41, 46) sts; turn and complete row.

Work 33 (38, 43) sts; turn and complete row.

Work 30 (35, 40) sts; turn and complete row.

Work 28 (33, 38) sts; turn and complete row.

Do not BO; place sts on a holder.

Work the other side the same way, reversing shaping to correspond.

RIGHT FRONT

With smaller circular, CO 55 (60, 65) sts. Work 13 (15, 17) rows in ribbing as for back. Change to larger circular and begin pattern on RS. Pm as indicated below.

Row 1: Sl 1 purlwise, k3, p2, work following Charts B, A, C, A, pm, knit to end of row. For charts, see Symbols Key on page 157.

Row 2: Sl 1 purlwise, k1, p2, (k2, p3) to marker, work pattern following Charts A, C, A, B. End k2, p2, k2.
Rep Rows 1-2 until back measures 17¼ (17¾, 18¼) in / 44 (45, 46) cm and you are on the same row for armhole as for back.

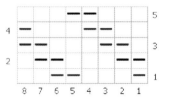

CHART B

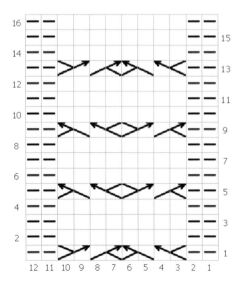

CHART A

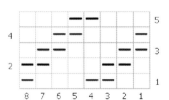

CHART C

JOINING THE SHOULDERS WITH RS FACING RS ALLOWS FOR SMOOTH PATTERN MATCHING

Shape armhole:
BO 7 sts at side with the garter columns and, on same side, CO 2 sts for new edge sts = 50 (55, 60) sts.

Continue as est, following chart until front measures 19 (19¾, 20½) in / 48 (50, 52) cm. Now begin shaping V-neck (with a total of 20 sts decreased on all sizes), *decreasing on WS rows:* When a total of 7 sts rem on row, k2tog, k1, p2, k2 (right-leaning decrease). Decrease the same way on every other row 18 times and then on every 4th row 2 times = 30 (35, 40) sts rem.

Work as est until front is same length as back (make it easy by counting the number of crosses or circles).
NOTE: On the last row, BO the 2 edge sts at neck edge = 28 (33, 38) sts rem. *Do not* bind off rem sts; place sts on a holder while you knit the left front.

LEFT FRONT
Work as for right front through Row 13 (15, 17). Change to larger circular and begin pattern on RS. Pm as indicated below.

Row 1: Sl 1 purlwise, k8 (13, 18), pm, work following chart sequence A, B, A, C, p2, k4 For charts, see Symbols Key on page 157.
Row 2: Sl 1 purlwise, k1, p2, k2; work pattern following charts C, A, B, A to marker; (p3, k2) until 4 sts rem and end p2, k2.

Rep Rows 1-2 until back measures 17¼ (17¾, 18¼) in / 44 (45, 46) cm and you are on the same row for armhole as for back.

Shape armhole:
BO 7 sts at side with the garter columns as before, and, on same side, CO 2 sts for new edge sts.

Continue as for right front, shaping V-neck on WS rows as follows: Sl 1 knitwise, k1, p2, k1, ssk (left-leaning decrease).

When left front matches right front at shoulder, BO the edge sts and leave rem sts on needle so you can join shoulders.

JOINING SHOULDERS

Place back and front with RS facing RS and join with 3-needle bind-off. Use an extra needle to k2tog with the first st from each needle; *join next st on each needle with k2tog and then pass st at right on right needle over left st (see page 134). Continue the same way from * until all 28 (33, 38) sts have been bound off at each shoulder. Cut yarn and draw end through rem st. Join opposite shoulder the same way.

SLEEVES (WORKED BACK AND FORTH)

With smaller circular, CO 50 (50, 50) sts.
Row 1 (WS): Sl 1 purlwise, k1, (p2, k2) to end of row.
Row 2: Sl 1 purlwise, k3, (p2, k2) until 2 sts rem, end k2.
Rep Rows 1-2 for a total of 11 (13, 15) rows.
With RS facing: There are 10 St st columns inside the outermost 6 sts at each side. Inc 1 st in each column with (k1, yo, k1) = 60 (60, 60) sts.
Next row: Work as for Row 2, working all yarnovers as p1tbl (twisting the yarnover before purling is easier).

Change to larger circular and begin working pattern on RS:
Rows 1 and 3: Sl 1 purlwise, k3, work charts A, C, A, B, A, end k4.
Rows 2 and 4: Sl 1 purlwise, k1, p2, work charts A, B, A, C, A until 4 sts rem, end p2, k2.
Row 5 (increase row): Sl 1 purlwise, k2, yo, work following charts until 3 sts rem, end with yo, k3.
Row 6 (WS): Sl 1 purlwise, work as est, with p1 tbl in each yarnover.

Continue as est, following chart sequence and increasing on every 4th row (the same row as cable crossings) until there are 102 (106, 110) sts. Check to be sure that the sleeves fit the armholes (most accurate fit is after shoulders have been joined) and adjust the number of increases as necessary. After completing increases, work without further shaping until sleeve is 17¾ (18¾, 19¾) in / 45 (47.5, 50) cm long or desired length. Finish with a couple of rows in St st for the seam allowance.

BO loosely so sleeve top doesn't pull in. Make second sleeve the same way.

BUTTON AND NECK BANDS

To ensure the k3, p2 ribbing will be even all around, the stitch count you pick up along the front edges should be a multiple of 5 sts + 3 (for example, 145 + 3 = 148 sts). (In the outer edges, there are 4 St sts instead of 3 because they will roll a little.) If you don't get the correct number of stitches when picking up, you can adjust the stitch count with increases or decreases when you work the first row.

With smaller circular, pick up and knit 143 (148, 153)) sts along right front edge inside the 2 edge sts, about 3

sts for every 4 rows. Work across the 44 back neck sts from holder, joining the "gaps" with the stitches on each side so they match the same ribbing as at lower edge: K1, (p2, k3) until 3 sts rem, p2, k1. Pick up and knit 143 (148, 153) sts along left front edge.
Row 1 (WS): P4, (k2, p3) until 6 sts rem and end k2, p4.
Rows 2 and 3: Work knit over knit and purl over purl.
Row 4 (buttonhole): The cardigan as shown in the photo has 6 buttons and 6 buttonholes. The lowest one is placed in the first purl column, and then they are spaced with 3 purl columns in between each. Decide which side you'd like to place the buttonholes on and how many of them you want, and mark the purl columns you will make them in.

There are various methods for making buttonholes. The easiest is to bind off 2-4 sts (depending on big the buttons are), and then cast on the same number of sts on the next row over the gap.

Continue in ribbing for a total of 7 rows. BO with knit over knit and purl over purl.

FINISHING

Attach sleeves. Sew the side and sleeve seams with mattress st (see page 135). Weave in all ends neatly on WS. Gently wash sweater in lukewarm water with wool-safe soap. Block by patting or pinning out garment to finished measurements; leave until completely dry. Sew on buttons.

YOU CAN SEE THE DIRECTION OF THE DECREASES ON THE WRONG SIDE MORE CLEARLY

WROUGHT IRON CARDIGAN

SKILL LEVEL EXPERIENCED
SIZES S (M, L)
FINISHED MEASUREMENTS
CHEST: 35½ (38½, 41¾) IN / 90 (98, 106) CM
LENGTH: 19¾ (21¾, 24) IN / 50 (55, 61) CM

MATERIALS
YARN:
CYCA #4 (WORSTED, AFGHAN, ARAN) CASCADE YARNS CASCADE 220 (100% PERUVIAN HIGHLAND WOOL, 220 YD/201 M / 100 G)
YARN AMOUNT AND COLOR:
5 (6, 7) SKEINS, COLOR HEATHERS 8013
NEEDLES U.S. SIZE 6 / 4 MM: 32 IN / 80 CM CIRCULAR + 1 EXTRA FOR BIND-ING OFF;

U.S. SIZE 4 / 3.5 MM: 24 OR 32 IN / 60 OR 80 CM CIRCULAR FOR NECK AND BUTTON BANDS; CABLE NEEDLE
NOTIONS STITCH MARKERS; BUTTONS; CROCHET HOOK FOR BUTTONHOLES
GAUGE
20 STS IN ST ST ON LARGER NEEDLES = 4 IN / 10 CM.
ADJUST NEEDLE SIZES TO OBTAIN CORRECT GAUGE IF NECESSARY.

IT'S POSSIBLE that I'm partial to split hems! The lower edges of the back and front pieces of this sweater are knitted separately to allow for split hems when the pieces are joined. The columns made with slipped stitches at the lower edges add extra sturdiness before they flow into the pattern motifs. When the split hem edge stitches are finished, they combine for a new column, and so a circle can appear even there.

On the flip side, I don't like partial pattern motifs much at all. One solution to this potential problem is to make different pattern repeats for different sizes, and that's what I've done here. You can choose the chart for your size.

Lena, one of my knitting friends, said this pattern reminded her of decorative wrought iron—and I had to agree. So I was given a name for the sweater, just like that!

WROUGHT IRON CARDIGAN

INFORMATION
Always hold the yarn in front when you slip one or two purl stitches.

LOWER BACK
With larger circular, CO 98 (106, 114) sts.
Row 1 (WS): Sl 2 purlwise, *k10 (11, 12), sl 2 purlwise*; rep * to * 7 times.
Row 2: Knit.

Rep these 2 rows until you've worked a total of 19 (21, 21) rows, ending with a WS row. Cut yarn and leave sts on a holder.

LOWER EDGE LEFT FRONT
With larger circular, CO 52 (56, 60) sts.
Row 1 (WS): Sl 1 purlwise, k1, p2, *k10 (11, 12), sl 2 purlwise*; rep * to * 3 times.
NOTE: The edge sts are worked differently at the two sides—towards the center, they are worked and slipped as for the back, but towards the front edge, only the outermost stitch is slipped.
Row 2: Knit.

Rep these 2 rows until you've worked a total of 19 (21, 21) rows, ending with a WS row. Cut yarn and leave sts on a holder.

LOWER EDGE RIGHT FRONT
With larger circular, CO 52 (56, 60) sts.
Row 1 (WS): *Sl 2 purlwise, k10 (11, 12)*; rep * to * 3 times; end p2, k2.
Row 2: Sl 1 purlwise, knit to end of row.

Rep these 2 rows until you've worked a total of 19 (21, 21) rows, ending with a WS row. **NOTE:** *Do not cut yarn.* On the next row, you will join the three pieces, beginning with right front.

JOINING THE THREE PIECES
With RS facing and right front, sl 1 purlwise, knit until 2 sts rem. Sl 1 knitwise, place st back on left needle so that it is twisted and then k2tog tbl (the decrease leans to the left).
Continue over the back: K2tog with first 2 sts (the decrease leans to the right), knit until 2 sts rem; twist the next-to-last st as above and k2tog tbl.
Finish with left front: K2tog, knit to end of row = 198 (214, 230) sts.
Next row: Sl 1 purlwise, k1, *p2, k10 (11, 12)*; rep * to * until 4 sts rem, end p2, k2.

Now work following chart for your size: S (M, L). (See Symbols Key on page 157.)

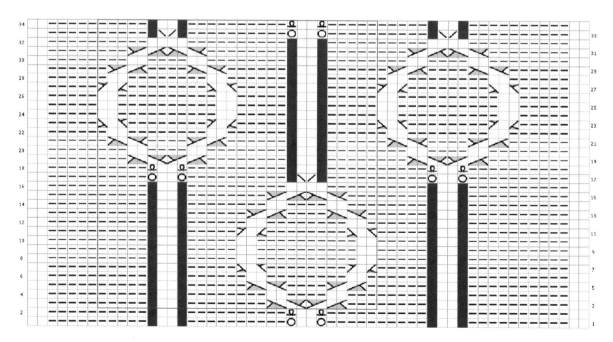

CHART FOR SIZE SMALL (S)

The first and last 2 sts of the row aren't included on the charts but should be worked as est: Sl 1 purlwise, k1; k2 at end of row. From the charts, work the red framed repeat 7 times. Work Rows 1-34 and 3-34 (1-38 and 3-38, 1-42 and 3-42) of chart. Now divide the work into 3 sections again.

RIGHT FRONT
With RS facing: Work all of Row 3 of chart, which shows all the sts of front across the width, minus the edge sts. Work the edge sts as est and then chart sts. End by casting on 2 new edge sts on the other side. Continue following the chart through Row 34 (38, 42) and then work Rows 3-8 (3-8, 3-10).
Shape neck: Continuing charted pattern, BO 9-5-3-3-3 (9-6-4-3-3; 9-7-4-4-3) sts at beginning of every other row. Then work through Row 24 (26, 30). *Do not* bind off; place rem 33 (35, 37) sts on a holder.

BACK
With RS facing, CO 2 new edge sts and work Row 3 of chart. Continue following the chart, working the repeat 3 (3, 3) times; end by casting on 2 new edge sts.
Turn and continue charted pattern + the edge sts at each side. (The edge sts are worked as for edges of front: sl 1 purlwise, k1, work chart sts, end k2.) Begin by working through Row 34 (38, 42) and then Rows 3-14 (3-16, 3-18).

Shape neck: Continue following chart, working 39 (41, 45) sts (including edge sts). Turn, BO 2 sts and complete row. BO 2 sts for neck on every other row until 33 (35, 37) sts rem. Work without further shaping through Row 24 (26, 30). *Do not* bind off; place rem sts on a holder. Shape the other side of back neck the same way, reversing shaping to correspond.

LEFT FRONT
With RS facing: CO 2 new edge sts and work Row 3 of chart. Work as for right front, reversing shaping for neck.

JOINING SHOULDERS
Place back and front with RS facing RS and join with 3-needle bind-off. Use an extra needle to k2tog with the first st from each needle; *join next st on each needle with k2tog and then pass st at right on right needle over left st (see page 134). Continue the same way from * until all sts have been bound off at each shoulder. Cut yarn and draw end through rem st. Join opposite shoulder the same way.

SLEEVES (MAKE BOTH ALIKE)
With larger circular, CO 48 (48, 54) sts.
Row 1 (WS): Sl 1 purlwise, k1 (= edge sts), p2, *k5 (5, 6), sl 2 purlwise*; rep * to * until 4 sts rem and end p2, k2 (= edge sts).

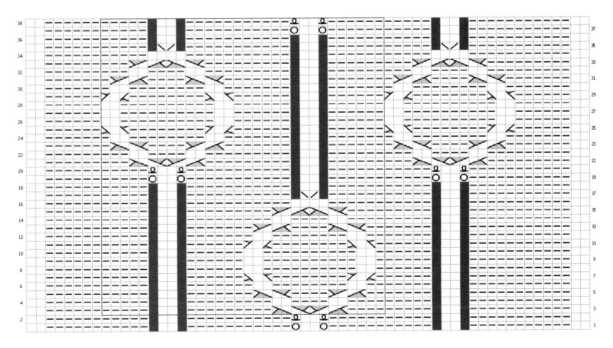

CHART FOR SIZE MEDIUM (M)

Row 2: Sl 1 purlwise, knit to end of row.

Rep these 2 rows until you've worked 19 (21, 21) rows total, ending with a WS row.

Now begin shaping sleeve with yarnovers and in St st against a reverse St st background as for front and back. Increase with yarnovers on every 4th row.

NOTE: The remaining instructions do not mention the 2 edge sts at each side but they are continued and worked as above throughout the sleeve.

Row 1: K2, p5 (5, 6), k2, p1, yo. Work knit over knit and purl over purl until 12 (12, 13) sts rem (including edge sts), yo, p1, k2, p5 (5, 6), k2.

Row 2: Work knit over knit and purl over purl, working yarnovers as k1tbl.

Rows 3 and 4: Work knit over knit and purl over purl.

Rep these 4 rows a total of 5 (6, 6) times = 58 (60, 66) sts. Now work increases closer to the edges.

Row 1 (all sizes): K2, p1, yo; work knit over knit and purl over purl until 5 (5, 5) sts rem (including edge sts) and end yo, p1, k2.

Row 2: Work knit over knit and purl over purl, working yarnovers as k1tbl.

Rows 3 and 4: Work knit over knit and purl over purl.

Rep these 4 rows until there are 80 (90, 100) sts. Measure sleeve top against armhole and adjust stitch count if necessary. After completing increases, work without further shaping until sleeve is 17¾ (18¾, 19¾) in / 45 (47.5, 50) cm long or desired length. Finish with a couple of rows in St st for the seam allowance.

BO rather loosely so sleeve top doesn't pull in.

NECKBAND

With RS facing and smaller circular: Pick up and knit 1 st in each st along right front and about 2 sts for every 3 rows along straight edge at shoulder. Work back sts from holder and then pick up and knit sts along left front as for right side.

Knit 7 rows in garter st. Change St st columns to slip sts on WS as for lower edge of sweater. BO.

BUTTON BANDS

With RS facing and smaller circular: Pick up and knit approx. 95 (105, 115) sts along one front edge, about 3 sts for every 4 rows. Knit 2 rows to stabilize edge and then BO. Edge the opposite front edge the same way. With crochet hook, make chain st button loops on one side (see photos).

FINISHING

Attach sleeves. Sew sleeve seams with mattress st (see page 135). Weave in all ends neatly on WS. Gently wash sweater in lukewarm water with wool-safe soap. Block by patting or pinning out garment to finished measurements; leave until completely dry. Sew on buttons.

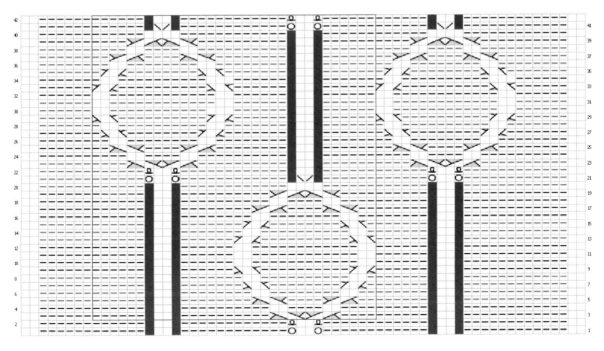

CHART FOR SIZE LARGE (L)

ARROW SWEATER

SKILL LEVEL EXPERIENCED
SIZE CHILD (S, M, L)
FINISHED MEASUREMENTS
CHEST: 31½ (36¾, 39½, 41¾) IN / 80 (93, 100, 106) CM
LENGTH: 19¾ (23, 24 ½, 24¾) IN / 50 (60, 62, 63) CM

MATERIALS
YARN:
CYCA #3 (SPORT) ÖSTERGÖTLANDS ULLSPINNERI VISJÖ (100% WOOL, 328 YD/300 M / 100 G)
YARN AMOUNT AND COLOR: 3 (4, 4, 5) SKEINS, OLIVE GREEN
NEEDLES U.S. SIZE 2.5 / 3 MM: 24 IN / 60 CM FOR CHILD'S SIZE; 32 IN / 80 CM FOR ADULT SIZES + 1 EXTRA FOR

JOINING; SET OF 5 DPN FOR SLEEVES; U.S. SIZE 1.5 / 2.5 MM: 16 IN / 40 CM CIRCULAR; CABLE NEEDLE
NOTIONS STITCH MARKERS
GAUGE
25 STS IN ST ST ON U.S. SIZE 2.5 / 3 MM NEEDLES = 4 IN / 10 CM. ADJUST NEEDLE SIZE TO OBTAIN CORRECT GAUGE IF NECESSARY.

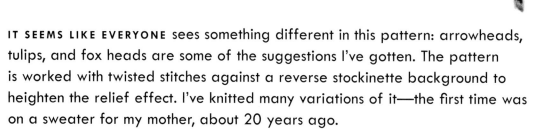

IT SEEMS LIKE EVERYONE sees something different in this pattern: arrowheads, tulips, and fox heads are some of the suggestions I've gotten. The pattern is worked with twisted stitches against a reverse stockinette background to heighten the relief effect. I've knitted many variations of it—the first time was on a sweater for my mother, about 20 years ago.

The sweater is constructed so the narrow cables on the lower edge either continue as a group or transition into other patterns. The half repeats, which end at the front and back pieces, also transform into a new block pattern over the shoulders. The neck is shaped with short rows so you can continue with the "resting" stitches and the pattern naturally flows to the ribbed edge. I love it when everything works out smoothly!

ARROW SWEATER

All the knit stitches on the chart are twisted (worked through the back loop) but I refrained from marking each with a special symbol. Twisting is easier on knit rather than purl stitches, so this sweater is worked in the round as much as possible.

The neckband is the only place without twisted knit stitches because it needs extra elasticity. Of course, you can work the design without any twisted stitches but that affects the gauge enough that the sizing will change. See the photo on page 148 comparing twisted and untwisted stitches.

Narrow cables are quite easy to knit without a cable needle! With the needle behind the first stitch, knit the second stitch into the back loop but do not drop it off the needle. Knit the first stitch through the back loop and slide both stitches off the needle.

BACK AND FRONT

With U.S. size 2.5 / 3 mm circular, CO 208 (240, 256, 272) sts. Join, being careful not to twist cast-on row. Pm for beginning of rnd. Work following Chart A (see Symbols Key on page 157).

Sizes Child and S: Work Rows 1-15 of chart.
Size M: Work Rows 1-4 of chart and then Rows 1-15.
Size L: Work Rows 1-8 of chart and then Rows 1-15.
Work Row 16 and then follow Chart A as below (depending on chosen size)
Child: *Work sts 1-40, 9-40, 9-40*; rep * to * = 5 cables on each side and 3 between arrows.
S: Work sts 1-40 6 times = 5 cables on each side and 5 between arrows.
M: *Work sts 1-8, 1-40, 1-40, 1-40*; rep * to * = 7 cables on each side and 5 between arrows.
L: *Work sts 1-16, 1-40, 1-40, 1-40*; rep * to * = 9 cables on each side and 5 between arrows.

Continue, following the chart through Row 47.
Rep Rows 16-47 until piece measures 13 (14¼, 14½, 15) in / 33 (36, 37, 38) cm. Now divide for back and front. Make sure the last row is an odd-numbered row so the cables cross on the RS as before. Cut yarn.

DIVIDE FRONT AND BACK

There is a group of 5 (5, 7, 9) cables at each side.
BO the center 10 (10, 10, 18) sts at each side for the

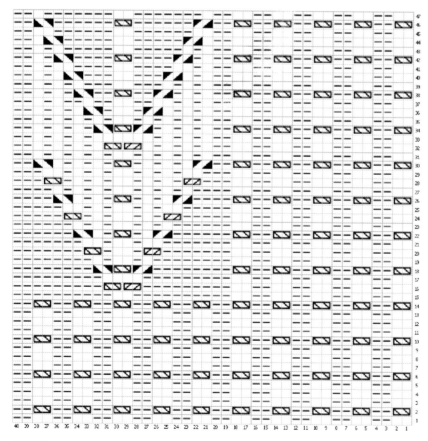

CHART A

THE NUMBER OF NARROW CABLES BETWEEN THE ARROWS DIFFERS ACCORDING TO SIZE

armhole shaping = 3 (3, 3, 5) cables and the purl sts between them.

Begin at the front: CO 2 sts for edge sts, work following chart on RS and end by casting on 2 edge sts = 98 (114, 122, 122) sts rem. The edge sts will be used for seaming and are worked the same way on both RS and WS: Sl 1 purlwise wyf, k1; end row with k2 edge sts. Work as est until there are 4 (5, 5, 5) complete arrows; end with Row 47.

Neck shaping: Shape neck with short rows (see pages 136-137) and following Chart B (C, C, C). Pm around the center 20 (36, 36, 36) sts.

On RS: Work to marker; turn and work back. The slipped st is indicated with Ȼ on the chart. Continue short row shaping on every other row as est until you've worked all the rows on the chart.

NOTE: Due to space restrictions, not all of the sts for the front are included on the chart—just enough so you can see where the turns occur = 26 (26, 30, 30) sts.

Do not BO, but, place rem sts on a holder. Shape the other side the same way, reversing shaping to correspond.

Work the back as for the front until there are 4 (5, 5, 5) complete arrows. Work another 8 rows (Rows 16-23 of Chart A). Pm around the center 36 (52, 52, 52) sts. Work short row shaping as for front, *but* follow Chart D (E, E, E). As for front, the charts do not include all the sts for the back—just enough so you can see where the

turns occur = 26 (26, 30, 30) sts. *Do not* BO; leave sts on needle for joining shoulders. Shape the other side the same way, reversing shaping to correspond. Leave rem sts on needle.

JOINING SHOULDERS
Place back and front with RS facing RS and join with 3-needle bind-off. Use an extra needle to k2tog with the first st from each needle; *join next st on each needle with k2tog and then pass st at right on right needle over left st (see page 134). Continue the same way from * until all 26 (26, 30, 30) sts have been bound off at each

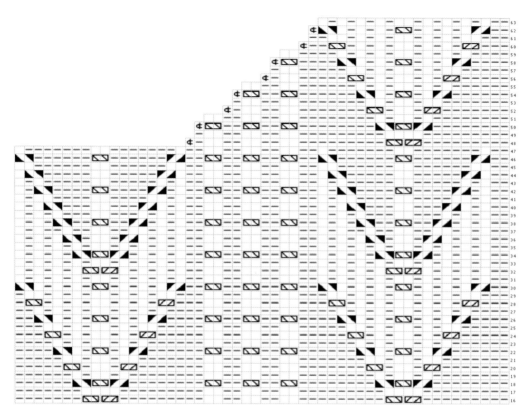

CHART B (THE FIRST ROW CORRESPONDS TO ROW 16 ON CHART A)

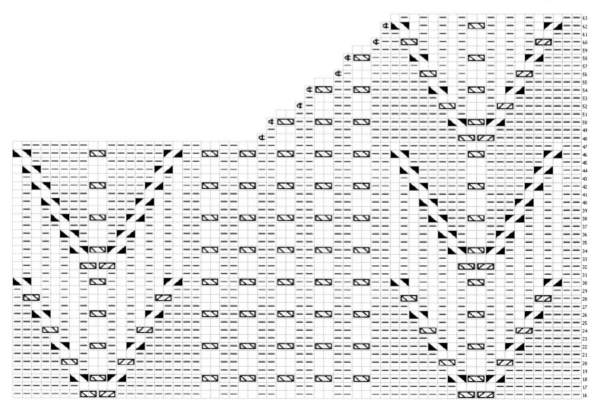

CHART C (THE FIRST ROW CORRESPONDS TO ROW 16 ON CHART A)

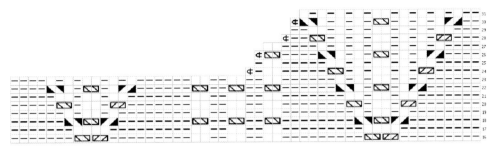

CHART D (THE FIRST ROW CORRESPONDS TO ROW 16 ON CHART A)

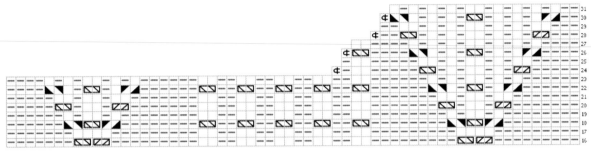

CHART E (THE FIRST ROW CORRESPONDS TO ROW 16 ON CHART A)

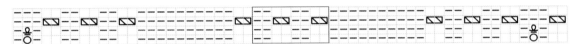

CHART F (SLEEVES, ALL SIZES)

shoulder. Cut yarn and draw end through rem st. Join opposite shoulder the same way.

NECKBAND
In my experience, it's a good idea to work the neckband before knitting the sleeves so you can try on your work and make sure it's the right size at a relatively early stage.

With RS facing and smaller circular, at left shoulder seam, pick up and knit 2 sts; work (p2, k2) across front. Pick up and knit 2 sts in right shoulder seam; (p2, k2) across back. Work a total of 6 (6, 8, 8) rnds k2, p2 ribbing and then BO.

SLEEVES (MAKE BOTH ALIKE)
With larger dpn, CO 56 (56, 64, 64) sts. Divide sts evenly onto 4 dpn; join, being careful not to twist cast-on row.

Work sleeve cuff following Rows 1-12 + 1-3 (1-12 + 1-3, 1-12, + 1-7, 1-12 + 1-7) of Chart A. Now begin sleeve shaping and following Chart F for St st sections.
Sizes M and L: Rep the section outlined in red once.

Increase with yarnovers; purling yarnovers through back loop on next rnd.

Continue working Chart F, increasing on every 8th (6th, 6th, 6th) rnd, with 1 st between the single cable to underarm until there are 80 (108, 116, 116) sts total. Make sure the sleeve fits well into the armhole—adjust shaping as necessary.

After completing increases, work without further shaping until sleeve is approx. 11¾ (17, 17¾, 18½) in / 30 (43, 45, 47) cm long or desired length minus ⅝ (⅝, ⅝, 1¼) in / 1.5 (1.5, 1.5, 3) cm. BO 2 st (= cable) and work another ⅝ (⅝, ⅝, 1¼) in / 1.5 (1.5, 1.5, 3) cm back and forth for finishing at armhole. End with a couple of rows in St st for seaming.

BO relatively loosely so the sleeve doesn't draw in.

FINISHING
Attach sleeves. Weave in all ends neatly on WS. Gently wash sweater in lukewarm water with wool-safe soap. Block by patting or pinning out garment to finished measurements; leave until completely dry.

HARMONY CARDIGAN

SKILL LEVEL EXPERIENCED
SIZES XS/S (M/L)
FINISHED MEASUREMENTS
CHEST: 37¾ (44) IN / 96 (112) CM
LENGTH: 21¾ (25½) IN / 55 (65) CM

MATERIALS
YARN:
CYCA #5 (BULKY) SANDNES FRITIDS-
GARN (100% WOOL, 77 YD/70 M /
50 G)
YARN AMOUNT AND COLOR:
12 (16) SKEINS, COLOR 2641 NATURAL
HEATHER (COLOR 2035 OCHRE)
NEEDLES U.S. SIZES 7 AND 8 / 4.5 AND
5 MM: CIRCULARS; CABLE NEEDLE

NOTIONS STITCH MARKERS; SMOOTH
COTTON SCRAP YARN OR EXTRA CIRCU-
LAR FOR SLEEVES; OPTIONAL: HOOKS
AND EYES
GAUGE
15 STS IN ST ST ON LARGER NEEDLES =
4 IN / 10 CM.
ADJUST NEEDLE SIZE TO OBTAIN COR-
RECT GAUGE IF NECESSARY.

RAGLAN SHAPING looks so good, and it's comfortable, too. Plus, if you work
a garment in one piece, you can place patterns where there would otherwise
be seams. This cardigan is worked from the top down, which makes it easy to
adjust the length. The only finishing is sewing the sleeve seams. The collar is
the same for both sizes, as is the transition to the yoke; but the larger size has
more raglan increases, so the yoke grows in both width and length.

Two more things affect the fit: a small gusset under each sleeve, and the
wavy endings of the lattice pattern. The latter yields more stockinette (stocking stitch) surface and automatically adds more width at the lower edge. If
you prefer a straighter shaping instead, you can continue working the lattice
across the entire width. The I-cord on the bottom edge matches up with that on
the front edges. If you want closures for the cardigan, you can sew on hooks
and eyes.

HARMONY CARDIGAN

There are obviously several patterns to work at the same time, but I've synchronized them to make it easier. Every sixth row, the cables cross in the narrow cords, as well as in the lattice and the cords in the large entwined cable pattern at center back. The pattern which repeats on the sleeves and front is broken out from the cable pattern. Compare Charts B and C below. (See the Symbols Key on page 157.)

BASIC INFORMATION

Edges (2 at each side): Always slip the first st purlwise with yarn in front on all rows. Always knit the 2nd st as well as the last 2 sts on all rows.

NOTE: The edge sts are only included on Rows 1-17 of the written instructions but continue the same way throughout.

COLLAR

The collar has wide St st and narrow garter st columns. They're shaped with short rows (see pages 136-137) to lengthen the collar at back neck.
With smaller circular, CO 90 sts.

Row 1 (WS): Sl 1 purlwise, k1 (= edge sts), p3, rep (k2, p4) 13 times until a total of 7 sts rem, k2, p3, k2 (= edge sts).

Row 2: Sl 1, knit to end of row.

Row 3: Work as for Row 1.

Row 4: Sl 1, knit until 24 sts rem; turn (see pages 136-137) and work Row 5.

Row 5: Work in pattern until a total of 24 sts rem; turn.

Row 6: Knit until a total of 18 sts rem; turn.

Row 7: Work in pattern until 18 sts rem; turn.

Row 8: Knit until a total of 12 sts rem; turn.

Row 9: Work in pattern until 12 sts rem; turn.

Row 10: Knit until a total of 6 sts rem; turn.

Row 11: Work in pattern until 6 sts rem; turn.

Row 12: Knit across.

Row 13: Sl 1 purlwise, work in pattern to end of row.

Row 14 (RS): Change to larger circular. Make 8 yarn-over increases as follows: Sl 1 purlwise, k10, yo, k2, yo, k28, yo, k2, yo, k4, yo, k2, yo, k28, yo, k2, yo, k11 = 98 sts.

Row 15: Work as for Row 1 with all yarnovers as k1tbl.

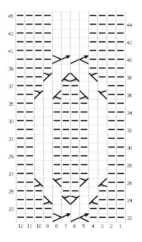

CHART A,
BEGIN ON ROW 16

CHART B,
BEGIN ON ROW 22

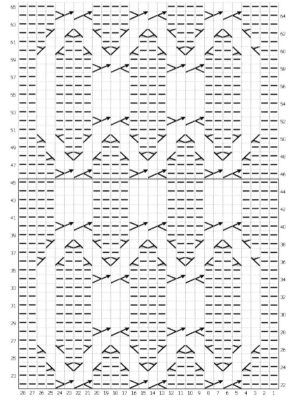

CHART C,
BEGIN ON ROW 22

DIVIDE FOR RAGLAN

Rnd 16: The cables (following only Chart A) and the raglan increases begin at the same time; the garter st sections now become reverse St st. Inside the outermost 7 sts at each edge will be 13 St st columns (all 4 sts wide). Counting from the right, pm at the 3rd, 5th, 9th, and 11th columns. From this point on, the raglan increases occur on each side of these columns, with a margin of 1 purl st. The increases are made in every other row with yarnovers on the RS.

Sl 1 st purlwise, k4, p2, work Chart A, p4, Chart A = **front**

P1, yo, p1, Chart A, p1, yo, p1 = **raglan cable with increases**

Chart A = **sleeve**

P1, yo p1, Chart A, p1, yo, p1 = **raglan cable with increases**

Chart A, p4, Chart A, p4, Chart A = **back**

P1, yo, p1, Chart A, p1, yo, p1 = **raglan cable with increases**

Chart A = **sleeve**

P1, yo, p1, Chart A, p1, yo, p1 = **raglan cable with increases**

Chart A, p4, Chart A, p2, k5 = **front**

NOTE: From this point onwards, unless otherwise specified, continue working edge sts as est.

Row 17: Between edge sts, work knit over knit and purl over purl, with all yarnovers as k1tbl.

Rows 18-21: Work knit over knit and purl over purl, *at the same time* increasing for raglan with yarnovers on RS: Work up to the purl st before the raglan cable, yo, p1, k4 (= raglan cable), p1, yo. Don't forget to work yarnovers as k1tbl on WS as on Row 17.

Rows 22-33:
NOTE: On Row 22, continue with Chart A for the front edges and raglan lines but change to Chart B for the fronts and sleeves, and Chart C for the back. The chart sequence is: A, B, A, B, A, C, A, B, A, B, A. *Don't forget the raglan increases* as you work the charts (see Rows 18-21).

Row 34: Work the 4th cable crossings and then add the reverse image lattice pattern (Charts D and E) on each side of the raglan cables.

A, B, D   = front
A   = raglan cable
E, B, D   = sleeve
A   = raglan cable
E, C, D   = back
A   = raglan cable
E, B, D   = sleeve
A   = raglan cable
E, B, A   = front

Work following the charts with increases as est through the row with the cable crossing labeled with a 9 (11) in the raglan cables. For the smaller size, this corresponds to Row 63 on Charts D and E. For the larger size, continue increasing and adding a block in width in the lattice pattern. Continue through Row 75: See Charts D2 and E2 for how to work the larger size through Row 64.

DIVIDING THE BODY

On Row 64 (76), stop the yoke increases. Divide the yoke into separate pieces at the center of the raglan cables and add stitches for the underarm gussets: Work 41 (53) sts of front following the chart (without any increases) and then k2 sts (raglan cable). Place 60 (72) sts on a holder for sleeve. CO 10 sts for underarm (see photo of gusset on page 129).

Work 76 (88) sts of back following chart (without increases) until you reach the next raglan cable. K2, place 60 (72) sts on holder and CO 10 sts for underarm. Work the 41 (53) sts of front following the chart (no increases). Continue working following the charts. For the smaller size, rep Rows 64-75 on charts D and E; for the larger size, rep Rows 76-87 on charts D2 and E2.

NOTE: Under each sleeve, work 14 sts for the gusset following Chart F in St st—the 10 cast-on sts + 2 sts at each side of raglan cables. The gusset sts will be decreased until 8 sts rem (the decreases are placed so that they are hidden by the cable pattern). Work cable crossings on the same row as those in Chart A. After completing charts, rep Rows 19-24.

The finished garment has a total of 5 (6) pattern repeats at center back. To shift the lattice pattern to a wavy edge as for the cardigan shown here, you need to prepare earlier: Start at the single block which begins the lattice and count straight down; when you have a total of 8 (9) blocks in a vertical line, end the outermost lines in a point at the center. See Chart G (XS/S) or G2 (M/L). They also show how to end Chart D (the lines cross mirror-image in E). The last row of these two charts is worked on the RS.

If, instead, you want a straight edge, continue with the lattice pattern as before until there are 5 (6) pattern repeats at center back. End with a RS row.

I-cord: Set-up with p2tog, purl until 2 sts rem and end p2tog; turn work. *K2, k2tog tbl, slide the 3 sts back to left needle* (see photo on page 84). Rep * to * across. Slide the 3 rem sts to left needle and k3tog. Cut yarn and draw end through last st.

SLEEVES

Place the 60 (72) sleeve sts on larger circular. With RS facing: CO 2 edge sts at beginning of row, work following chart and end with CO 2 edge sts = 64 (76) sts. Work edge sts as est.

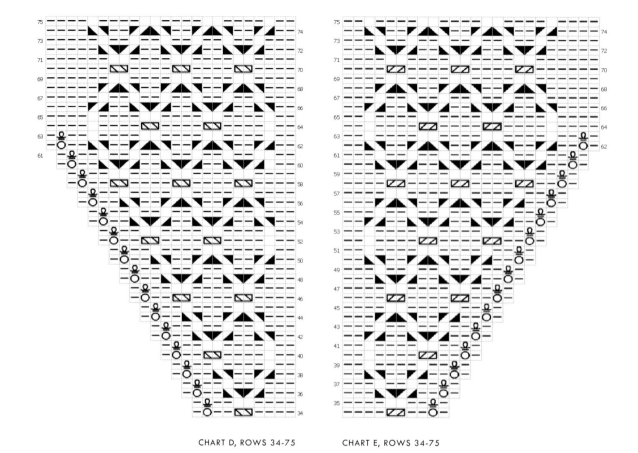

CHART D, ROWS 34-75   CHART E, ROWS 34-75

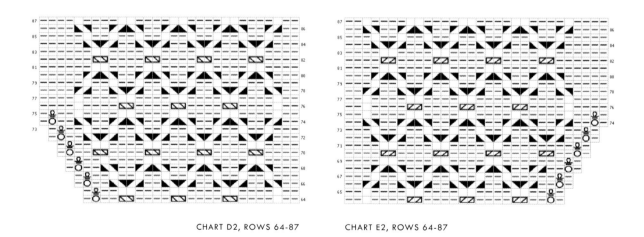

CHART D2, ROWS 64-87   CHART E2, ROWS 64-87

128

Work another 6 rows following the chart and then begin decreasing on WS: Join the 5th and 6th sts (counting edge sts) with ssk. Continue across until 6 sts rem, k2tog, p2, k2. Decrease the same way on every 6th row, always on WS (the row after the lattice lines have crossed). Check the sleeve length and adjust the rate of decreasing with more or fewer rows between decrease rows as necessary.

Work until 40 sts rem and then begin the cuff, which has the same pattern as the collar. On RS: Sl 1 purlwise and then knit to end of row. On WS: Sl 1 purlwise, k1, p2, (k2, p4) until 6 sts rem and end k2, p2, k2. Work another 11 rows as est or to desired length. With WS facing, BO in the same pattern as the knit and purl sts. Work the second sleeve exactly the same way.

FINISHING

Seam the sleeves with mattress stitch (see page 135). Sew the front edge sts to the inside if you think it is necessary. Weave in all ends neatly on WS. Gently wash sweater in lukewarm water with wool-safe soap. Block by patting or pinning out garment to finished measurements; leave until completely dry. If desired, sew on hooks and eyes for closure.

NEW STITCHES FOR A GUSSET UNDER THE SLEEVE (SEE CHART F)

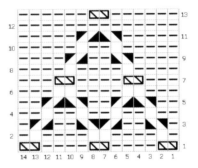

CHART G1, TIP OF LATTICE XS/S

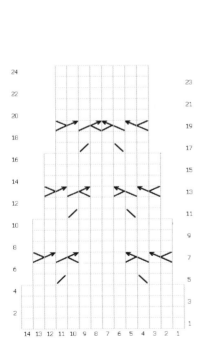

CHART F

CHART G2, TIP OF LATTICE M/L

KNITTING TECHNIQUES

CABLE KNITTING

The basic principle of cable knitting is simple: The stitches change places, and are twisted across the surface of the fabric. A useful tool is a cable needle, available in several styles. To cross a cable, for example, slip two stitches to the cable needle, hold them in front or in back of the work (depending on which direction the cable will lean), work one or more stitches from the left needle, and then work the stitches on the cable needle.

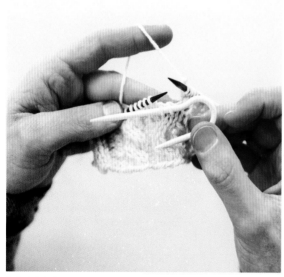

1. SLIP 2 STS TO CABLE NEEDLE AND HOLD CABLE NEEDLE IN FRONT OF WORK

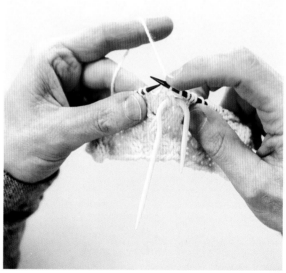

2. KNIT 2 STS ON LEFT NEEDLE

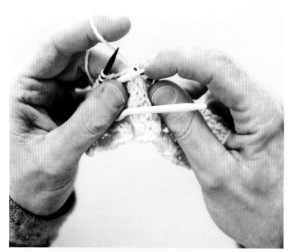

3. KNIT 2 FROM CABLE NEEDLE

4. THE CABLE CROSS LEANS TO THE LEFT

THREE-NEEDLE BIND-OFF (3-NDL BO)

This is a neat finishing technique that joins two pieces by binding off the stitches of both pieces at the same time. The technique produces different effects depending on how the pieces face each other. For pattern work, I like to have the wrong sides facing out (such as the shoulder joins for the Wrought Iron Cardigan, see page 115). For a decorative edge, I work with the right sides facing out (as for the Appearances Can Deceive sweater on page 83). You'll need 3 needles for 3-needle bind-off, two to hold the stitches and a third to work with.

1. INSERT THE NEEDLE THROUGH TWO STS, ONE FROM EACH NEEDLE

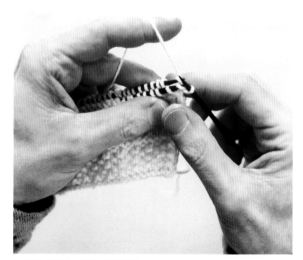

2. KNIT THESE 2 STS TOGETHER AND SLIP THEM OFF NEEDLE

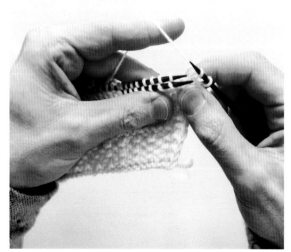

3. REPEAT STEPS 1 AND 2

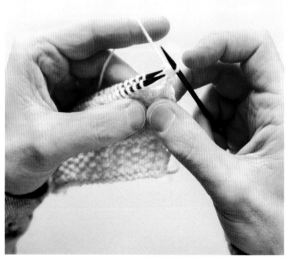

4. PASS THE RIGHT STITCH OVER THE LEFT ONE

MATTRESS STITCH

This is my favorite way of sewing together the side and sleeve seams. With right sides facing out, you can clearly see your place and can pull the work and yarn to adjust the stitches. It makes an invisible seam.

I usually begin and end by sewing 1 st in each st and then through two at a time. A bent-tip tapestry needle also makes the work easier. (For the sake of clarity here, I've used a contrast color strand.)

1. INSERT THE NEEDLE DOWN THROUGH A STITCH AND THEN UPWARDS TO THE STITCH ABOVE.

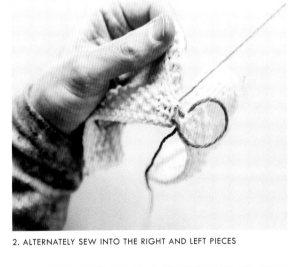

2. ALTERNATELY SEW INTO THE RIGHT AND LEFT PIECES

3. CONTINUE TO SEW THE ENTIRE SEAM, TIGHTENING IT AS YOU WORK

4. ON THE WRONG SIDE, THE SEAM LIES FLAT

SHAPING

SHORT ROWS

A practical way to shape knitting—for example, a neckline—is to work short rows. For this technique, you turn the work before a row is complete instead of binding off stepwise. Short rows yield a more even result; you avoid the "stairsteps" that form from the standard method of binding off. With this technique, you can continue knitting the live stitches instead of picking up new ones, which results in a neat finish. To avoid ugly holes at the turns,

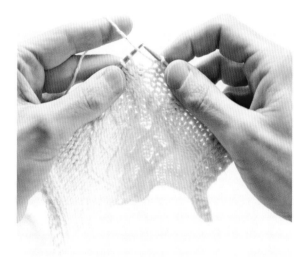

1. BRING YARN TO FRONT OF WORK

2. INSERT NEEDLE AS IF TO PURL

3. SLIP A STITCH WITH YARN STILL IN FRONT OF WORK

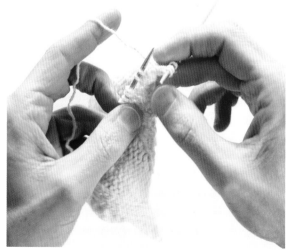

4. TAKE YARN TO BACK

it's a good idea to add a wrap around the stitch near the turn. Be careful not to pull too hard and strangle the stitch. On the next row, you can slip the st and work it together with the wrap—this is the most common when working in stockinette (stocking stitch). For garter stitch, I don't think the wrap is necessary because it practically disappears between the purl stitches.

5. TURN WORK

6. INSERT NEEDLE IN SAME STITCH AS IF TO PURL

7. SLIP STITCH WITH YARN STILL IN FRONT

8. CONTINUE WORKING

SAMPLE PATTERNS

ON THE FOLLOWING PAGES, I've collected a number of cable patterns with the idea that the section should function as a step-by-step school, a pattern collection, and a source of inspiration. Below you can see three simple variations of the same cable crossing—the only thing that differentiates them is the number of rows between cable crossings.

A pattern dictionary follows with combinations of two reverse-image cables. Next are pattern shapes that move sideways over a reverse stockinette background, columns that are similar to true cables, various figures against a stockinette background and, finally, comparison of the same patterns with and without twisted stitches.

The Symbols Key that explains the symbols on the charts can be found on page 157.

CROSSING CABLES AT DIFFERENT INTERVALS

Many cable patterns are built on stockinette columns over, for example, four stitches, where the stitches change places two by two. If the cables are set against purl stitches, the pattern becomes more obvious and the ribbed effect is enhanced.

The distance between cable crossing rows influences both the look and the gauge—the more closely the crossings are spaced, the firmer the pattern. Closer crossings also draw the knitting in more, which means it takes more yarn to work a piece with lots of close crossings than a piece of the same size with more distance between crossings.

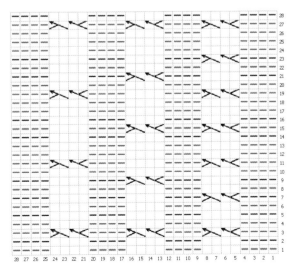

PATTERN 1: RIGHT, LEFT, ZIGZAG

When the cable needle is held in front of the work, the cable leans to the left; with the cable needle behind the work, the cable leans to the right. You can be consistent or alternate between left and right.

Alternating in a zigzag pattern elongates the piece and doesn't draw in the work as much as using only right- or left-leaning cables.

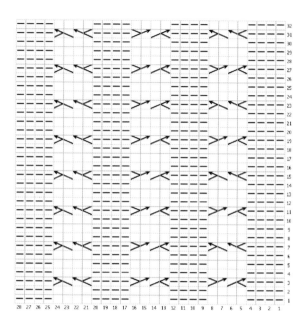

PATTERN 2: HORSESHOES

With the two crossings above, over four stitches each and leaning to the right or left, many new combinations can be created. By joining two columns (a total of 8 stitches), with mirror-image crossings, one can make a horseshoe-like

pattern, which can face upward or downward. See the next two patterns to the right for more possible combinations.

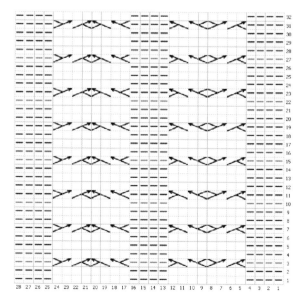

PATTERN 3: HONEYCOMB AND CHAIN

Another way to use mirror-image diagonals over eight stitches is to let them lean alternately to the right and left to form a chain pattern. Join two such patterns (a total of 16 stitches) and it becomes a honeycomb-like design.

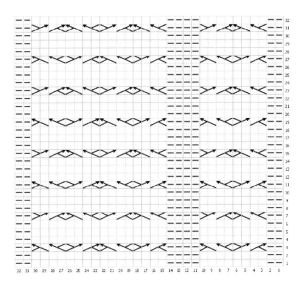

PATTERN 4: X AND O

The next step can be to make mirror-image leanings two times before changing direction. Over eight stitches an X-and-O pattern develops. You can also join columns here.

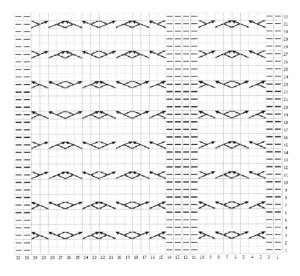

PATTERN 5: STEEP DIAGONAL

You can also move the lines sideways—for example, by moving the knit stitches over a reverse stockinette background. Two knit stitches over a purl stitch make a steep diagonal.

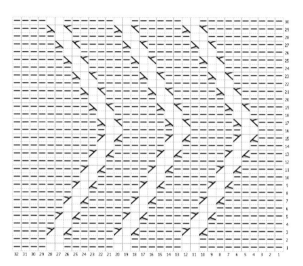

PATTERN 6: SIDEWAYS DIAGONAL

If you cross two knit stitches over two purl stitches, the columns bend further sideways and the fabric pulls in more.

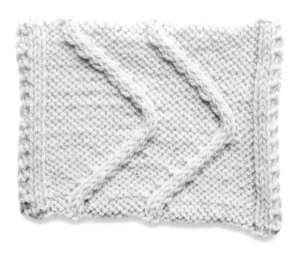

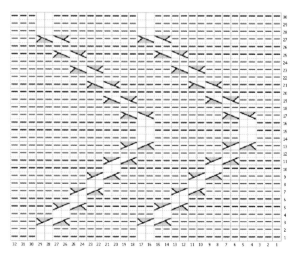

PATTERN 7: CIRCLE

By combining steep and sideways diagonals, you can form a circle. The degree to which the fabric will pull in depends on how many stitches are involved, but it can even out with increases and decreases.

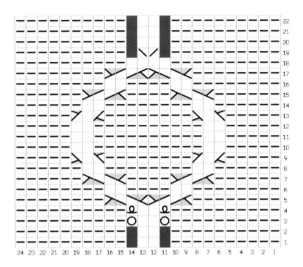

PATTERN 8: DIAMOND

You can also divide a pattern column into several narrower ones. In this pattern, the cable crossings occur in the center, on the wrong side.

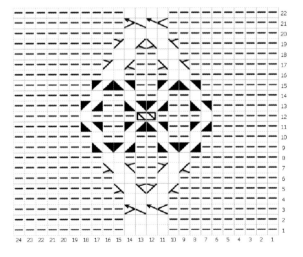

PATTERN 9: LATTICE

Individual shapes can be joined into a larger pattern.
Here, two knit stitches change places with one purl stitch.
When four knit stitches land next to each other, they
cross in pairs.

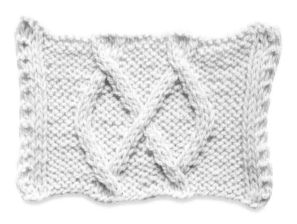

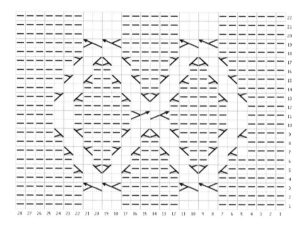

PATTERN 10: KNOTTED LATTICE

You can alter the lattice pattern by making two crossings
before the knit stitches divide again.

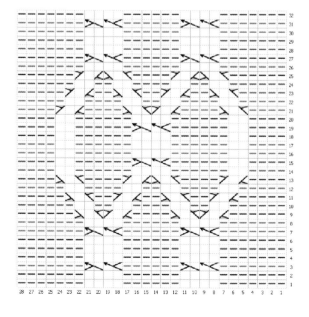

PATTERN 11: TWO TRIPLE CABLES

A stockinette column can also consist of three sections, similar to a braid.

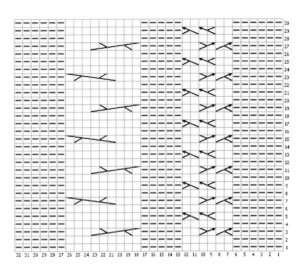

PATTERN 12: THREE BROKEN TRIPLE CABLES

If you break up a triple cable with sections without any cable crossings, another pattern appears.

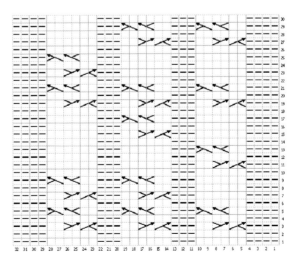

PATTERN 13: DIAGONAL LINES (STOCKINETTE BACKGROUND)

Of course, you can also work with an entirely stockinette surface. The diagonals are more obvious than on a reverse stockinette background.

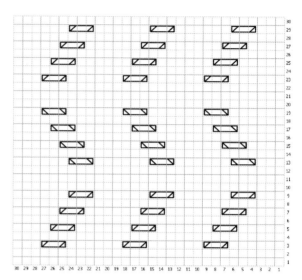

PATTERN 14: FOUR-LEAFED CLOVER (STOCKINETTE BACKGROUND)

Individual pattern shapes can be grouped into a larger one or spread over an entire surface.

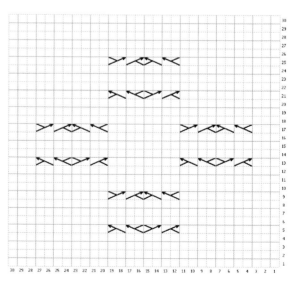

PATTERN 15: DIAGONAL LINES (STOCKINETTE BACKGROUND)

Pattern shapes can pull in the stockinette background so it "ripples." A smaller and rounder variation can be seen in the Figure Eights vest on page 102.

You can also see on the vest that it's possible to make a circular form by working half the chart.

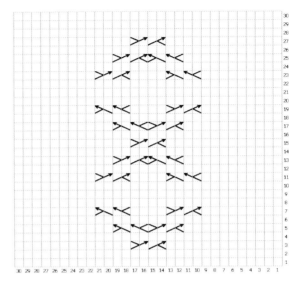

PATTERN 16: TREE (STOCKINETTE BACKGROUND)

Why not combine varying wide and long lines into a new pattern shape?

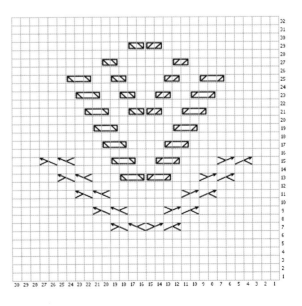

PATTERN 17: ARROW

Single knit stitches can form clear relief shapes if they're twisted (knit through the back loop). Here, the same pattern is first worked with regular knit stitches and then (below) with twisted knit stitches.

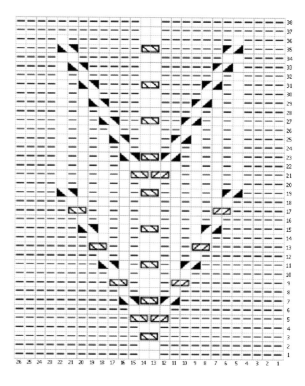

PATTERN 18: ARROW (TWISTED)

If all the knit stitches are twisted, the gauge changes because the fabric pulls in.

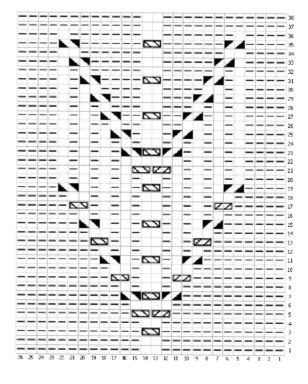

CHOOSING MATERIALS

As is always the case with knitting, it's a good idea to take your time when you're choosing yarn for a special project, to help ensure the end result will turn out the way you want. When it comes to cable patterns, there are a few factors to keep at the back of your mind when choosing among all the fibers and colors. It would be a shame to put in the time and effort to knit an intricate pattern, only to find it doesn't show up half as clearly as you'd like. And of course that also means it would take even longer to knit the project in the first place, because you wouldn't be able to see the pattern clearly as you went, and it would be all too easy to lose your place.

THE YARN COLOR PLAYS A ROLE
Cable patterns bring out shadows and texture effects, and are most distinctive with light, smooth single-color yarns. That doesn't mean other yarns can't be considered, but it's good to be aware of all the elements influencing how clearly a cable pattern will show. If the yarn is dark, the raised cables won't stand out as much. Yarn with a halo—mohair, for example—obscures the contours of a cable design. Similarly, the flecks in tweed yarns tend to make cables blend into the background. So I consider these yarns most suited to large pattern shapes. If you like self-striping yarn, consider how the color changes will overshadow the pattern structure; with those yarns, the cables disappear among the stripes or shades.

DIFFERENT YARNS BEHAVE DIFFERENTLY
You can actually get a very good idea of how a cable pattern will look by pulling out a few strands of yarn and examining them. If the yarn's round and elastic, the cables will have a chunky, bulky look; if it's flat and inelastic, the cables will be smaller and smoother. Whichever look it is you want your cables to have, keep it in mind as you choose materials.

A PRETTY YARN BUT TWEEDY, A LITTLE FLUFFY, AND RATHER DARK—
WHERE DID THE CABLES GO?

MORE ABOUT CHOOSING MATERIALS

Hopefully, as time passes, we all become not only older but wiser. When I was younger, I never thought much about where yarn came from; the only considerations in my mind were how much I liked it and whether I had enough money to buy it. I still consider those factors—but I also think about how much nicer it is to work with yarns that haven't been shipped all over the globe, and come to me from landscapes closer to home.

For some of the projects in this book, I used two yarns, Visjö and Renemo, that both come from Östergötlands Ullspinneri, a wool mill I've been able to visit in person and shop at happily as I worked on this book. For me, it lends the yarn a little something special when I get to see both where and how it's produced, and I have the chance to meet the people behind the materials. We should also be thankful for—and work to save—the wool mills and spinneries we have, old and new. Perhaps there's one near you? I'd like to list all the ones I'm familiar with, but I risk leaving one out!

It gives me such a feeling of closeness when I'm able to handle yarn at a mill. Just think: the skeins go directly from the hands that have processed the wool to the hands which, in their turn, will work with the yarn, without any detours through an unknown number of anonymous middlemen!

ULLA-KARIN AND BÖRJE AT ÖSTERGÖTLANDS WOOL MILL

YARN RESOURCES

To make comparisons easier, I've listed the yardage/meterage for each yarn as the amount in 100 g even if the yarn is sold in 25 g or 50 g balls.

BOMULD OG ULD—GEILSK
508 yd/464 m / 100 g (CYCA #1, fingering)
55% wool, 45% cotton
www.geilsk.dk

CASCADE 220—CASCADE YARNS
220 yd/201 m / 100 g (CYCA #4, worsted, afghan, aran)
100% Peruvian Highland wool
www.cascadeyarns.com

CYRANO—DE RERUM NATURA
164 yd/150 m / 100 g (CYCA #4, worsted, afghan, aran)
100% Merino wool
www.dererumnatura.fr

FRITIDSGARN—SANDNES
154 yd/140 m / 100 g (CYCA #5, bulky)
100% wool
www.sandnesgarn.no

GILLIATT—DE RERUM NATURA
273 yd/250 m / 100 g (CYCA #4, worsted, afghan, aran)
100% Merino wool
www.dererumnatura.fr

KARELEN—NORDISK ANGORA
273 yd/250 m / 100 g (CYCA #4, worsted, afghan, aran)
50% lamb's wool, 50% Angora rabbit
www.angora.se

RIOS—MALABRIGO YARNS
210 yd/192 m / 100 g (CYCA #4, worsted, afghan, aran)
100% superwash Merino wool
www.malabrigoyarn.com

NOVA—LANG YARNS
788 yd/720 m / 100 g (CYCA #3, sport)
48% Merino wool, 32% camel, 20% nylon
www.langyarns.com

RENEMO—ÖSTERGÖTLANDS ULLSPINNERI
219 yd/200 m / 100 g (CYCA #4, worsted, afghan, aran)
100% wool
www.ullspinneriet.se

VISJÖGARN—ÖSTERGÖTLANDS ULLSPINNERI
328 yd/300 m / 100 g (CYCA #3, sport)
100% wool
www.ullspinneriet.se

YAKU – CAMAROSE
438 yd/400 m / 100 g (CYCA #1, fingering)
100% superwash Merino wool
www.camarose.dk

A VARIETY OF ADDITIONAL AND SUBSTITUTE YARNS ARE AVAILABLE FROM:
Webs—America's Yarn Store
75 Service Center Road
Northampton, MA 01060
800-367-9327
yarn.com

LoveKnitting.com
loveknitting.com/us

If you are unable to obtain any of the yarn used in this book, it can be replaced with a yarn of a similar weight and composition. Please note, however, the finished projects may vary slightly from those shown, depending on the yarn used. Try www.yarnsub.com for suggestions.

For more information on selecting or substituting yarn, contact your local yarn shop or an online store; they are familiar with all types of yarns and would be happy to help you. Additionally, the online knitting community at Ravelry.com has forums where you can post questions about specific yarns. Yarns come and go so quickly these days and there are so many beautiful yarns available.

ABBREVIATIONS AND SYMBOLS KEY

ABBREVIATIONS

BO	bind off (UK = cast off)
CDD	centered double decrease = slip 2 sts together as if to knit, k1, psso
cm	centimeter(s)
CO	cast on
dpn	double-pointed needles
est	established (i.e., work as set up)
in	inch(es)
k	knit
k2tog	knit 2 sts together = 1 stitch decreased; right-leaning decrease
m	meter(s)
mm	millimeters
p	purl
p2tog	purl 2 sts together = 1 st decreased
pm	place marker
psso	pass slipped stitch(es) over
rem	remain(s)(ing)
rep	repeat
rnd(s)	round(s)
RS	right side
sl	slip
ssk	(sl 1 knitwise) 2 times; place sts back onto left needle and knit the stitches together through back loops = 1 stitch decreased; left-leaning decrease
st(s)	stitch(es)
St st	stockinette stitch (UK = stocking stitch)
tbl	through back loop(s)
WS	wrong side
wyb	with yarn held in back
wyf	with yarn held in front
yd	yard(s)
yo	yarnover

SYMBOLS EXCLUDING CABLE CROSSINGS

- k on RS, purl on WS
- p on RS, knit on WS
- no stitch
- yarnover
- twisted knit (= knit through back loop)
- twisted purl (= purl through back loop)
- sl 1 st purlwise with yarn held in front
- k2tog
- ssk = (sl 1 knitwise) 2 times; place sts back onto left needle and knit the stitches together through back loops
- p2tog
- with yarn held in front, sl 1 purlwise, bring yarn between needle tips; turn and sl the same stitch purlwise

SYMBOLS KEY FOR KNIT STITCH CABLE CROSSINGS

- Slip 1 st to cable needle and hold in back of work; k1, k1 from cable needle
- Slip 1 st to cable needle and hold in front of work; k1, k1 from cable needle
- Slip 1 st to cable needle and hold in back of work; k2, k1 from cable needle
- Slip 2 sts to cable needle and hold in front of work; k1, k2 from cable needle
- Slip 2 sts to cable needle and hold in back of work; k2, k2 from cable needle
- Slip 2 sts to cable needle and hold in front of work; k2, k2 from cable needle
- Slip 3 sts to cable needle and hold in back of work; k3, k3 from cable needle
- Slip 3 sts to cable needle and hold in front of work; k3, k3 from cable needle

SYMBOLS KEY FOR KNIT AND PURL STITCH CABLE CROSSINGS

- Sl 1 st to cable needle and hold in back of work; k1, p1 from cable needle
- Sl 1 st to cable needle and hold in front of work; p1, k1 from cable needle
- Sl 1 st to cable needle and hold in back of work; k2, p1 from cable needle
- Sl 2 sts to cable needle and hold in front of work; p1, k2 from cable needle
- Sl 2 sts to cable needle and hold in back of work; k2, p2 from cable needle
- Sl 2 sts to cable needle and hold in front of work; p2, k2 from cable needle

157

INDEX

ACKNOWLEDGMENTS

THANK YOU

First and foremost, the Swedish publisher's editorial team:
Annika for her indispensable eagle eye and beneficial
    encouragement.
Eva for the good ideas in her questions about everything
    from the details to the complete work, and for test-knitting
    patterns.
Tina for her infectious, sunny humor, not to mention the fantastic
    photography.
Mikael for unbelievable commitment and unbeatable taste in
    everything, big and small.

A big thank you also to:
Johanne for her friendship and professional proofreading.
Mette, Alexandra, Alva, Olga, Judit, and Anita for giving the
    garments life.
Kristinehovs Målmgard for letting us use the lovely rooms.
Doris for help with transportation—and laughter.
Ulla-Karin and Börje for the welcoming visits.

Last but not least:
Family and friends, of course!